SUCCESSFUL STAND-UP COMEDY

SUCCESSFUL STAND-UP COMEDY

Advice from a Comedy Writer

gene perret

SAMUEL FRENCH

HOLLYWOOD ✶ NEW YORK ✶ LONDON ✶ TORONTO

First Edition 1994

Library of Congress Cataloging-in-Publication Data

Perret, Gene
Successful stand-up comedy : advice from a comedy writer /
Gene Perret.
p.   cm.
1. Stand-up comedy—Vocational guidance. I. Title.
PN1969.C65P47   1994   792.7'023—dc20   94-13671

ISBN: 0-573-69916-X

Cover design by Heidi Frieder

Printed and bound in the United States of America

Published and distributed by
Samuel French Trade
7623 Sunset Blvd.
Hollywood, CA 90046

To Phyllis Diller

*who made good things happen
at the start of my comedy career*

CONTENTS

INTRODUCTION

When Bob Hope was invited to do a Command Performance commemorating the twenty-fifth anniversary of Queen Elizabeth's coronation, Bob Mills, Gig Henry, and I travelled with him to England as writers.

Moments before the show, I sat backstage at the Palladium Theatre as Hope went through a final glance at his opening monologue. The cue-card guys would quickly flip the cards, and Hope would mumble the line to himself, giving each joke a final approval and a quick rehearsal at the same time.

At one point he stopped the procedure and waved the card off. "Get rid of that joke," he said. It was my joke.

I said, "Bob, why are you getting rid of that? It's a funny joke."

The Queen's first grandchild had been born just a few months before, so we had some gags about royal baby-sitting and diaper changing. This was one of the "nappy" jokes ("nappy" being the British term for diapers). Hope felt it was too graphic.

"That's too rough for the Queen."

I objected. "The Queen will love that joke." (Like I know what Queen Elizabeth likes and doesn't like.)

Hope relented, though, picked up the card and studied it again.

"Do you think the Queen would really enjoy this joke?"

I said, "Sure she will."

He tossed the cue card to me and said, "Then you do it."

Hope was kidding me, of course, but his taunt did illustrate a show-business fact of life—writing is different from performing. Writers don't experience nearly the same jeopardy as performers. Writers don't get onstage and live or die by that performance. Hope was right. I didn't have to stand there and deliver a questionable joke before a ruler who, for all I knew, still had the power to behead.

If the gag fails, the entertainer's stomach drops a foot or two, the flop-sweat starts. The writer feels some disappointment, too, but he or she can retreat discreetly, can disappear to the nearest bar.

Some talk-show host once asked George Carlin if he used to be the class clown in school. He honestly admitted that he didn't have that kind of courage. He wasn't bold enough to fool around in class. However, he said that he did tell the class clown what to do.

That's what a writer is—a cowardly person who tells the talent what to do and say. We pack the parachute; the talent jumps out of the plane.

None of this implies that writers don't care. They do. I've worked with people who write nightclub material for comics, I've written on staffs for television variety shows, I've supervised writers on sitcoms, and I can guarantee that ninety-nine percent of them take enormous pride in what they put on paper. Even beyond that, they care about what goes on the air. They want the writing to be crisp; they want the telecast to sparkle; they want to feel an inner glow when their name slides by on the screen.

Writers are fiercely devoted to their craft and take their assignments seriously. Nevertheless, they still can't experience that do-or-die commitment. They don't get on the stage and live the words on the paper.

People often ask writers, "Who makes the final decision about material? Is it the writer or the comedian?" My answer is always the same: Whoever stands on the stage makes the decision.

I tell writers that they should perform their own comedy material at least once somewhere, somehow. I suggest that they speak at a PTA meeting, or deliver a short monologue to the Rotary club, or try an open-mike night at a comedy club. "Do it once," I tell them, "and you'll never get complacent about your material again. You'll know what it feels like to stand up there and suffer when the material isn't up to par."

We should confront one show-business fallacy here—that the writer-performer relationship is adversarial. It isn't, or rather I should say it needn't be.

Some performers do think they are the sole reason for a show's success, and to be fair, some writers think they are. Both are wrong.

I've often said that I've been writing comedy for thirty years and I've never written anything funny. Many of my confreres accept that statement at face value, but I'd prefer to explain it further. The words that I write are lifeless on paper. They have no soul, no heartbeat. Bob Hope has to give the words his inimitable delivery followed by that hint of a sneer. Phyllis Diller has to toss the words out to her audience and then highlight them with that raucous laugh. Carol Burnett says them with a funny take. Bill Cosby adds his style. Then the words come alive.

Comedy is a blend of material and performance. Each needs the other.

The writer is not the performer's foe. The writer is an ally, and a valuable one, too. I recall one time when there was a serious discussion about some material on the Bob Hope Show. Hope turned to me and said, "What do you think?"

I didn't relish being put on the spot like that, so I tried

to reason my way out of it. I said, "Bob, what's the difference what I think? You're the star of the show. You're going to win all the arguments."

I did it as a semi-serious joke, but he didn't laugh. He said, "Don't ever think like that. I need the input of my writers."

Jack Benny was the guest of honor at a Friars' Roast and naturally was lambasted with the insult humor that the Friars are famous for. When Jack stood up for his rebuttal, he said, "You wouldn't have said those things if my writers were here."

Professional comics have learned to use their writers for more than just putting words on paper. They offer much more input than that. They assist in creating new concepts, analyzing the pace of a performance, suggesting changes in format, keeping an eye out for nuances that the performer can't notice from the stage.

Performers have to devote their energies during a performance to performing. That's their job, and it takes more than talent. It takes effort and concentration. Regardless how attuned they are to things around them, they must primarily devote their energies to themselves, to their entertaining. Some subtleties must necessarily escape them. A writer in the wings who is once-removed from the emotionalism of the show can give a much more dispassionate analysis of a particular show.

An associate can view the performance from many different angles, whereas performers can only see from behind the microphone. An aide can watch from the wings, can view the show from the back of the auditorium, can mingle with the crowd before, during, and after the performance, and can gather critical information. He or she can reconnoiter for the entertainer.

That's the basic purpose of this book—to give you, the aspiring comedian, some of the input that I've gathered as the accomplice in the wings.

I've been doing it for over thirty years in nightclubs, concert work, and on TV. I've watched, worked with, and auditioned many comics. Some of the up-and-coming comedians I recommended for shows have gone on to become major stars; some I fought vehemently against have also gone on to become major stars.

Comedy is your business, so this book won't presume to tell you how to be funny. The author won't give you line readings or tell you which jokes to use or what style to adopt.

Comedy is so unpredictable that there is no way to tell what will or won't be funny tomorrow. Any style, even an unorthodox one, can be the standard of the next wave of comics.

This book offers observations that should apply universally to comedy acts, regardless of your style. In fact, some of the comments may be so basic that you might say, "Why even put that in writing?" These comments are included for those who may not be as advanced as you are. Just read over those and go on to the next plateau.

Some of the comments simply may not apply to you. I've tried to be universal, but that's not always possible. If I'm talking about projecting your voice so that it can be heard by all in the theatre and you're doing a pantomime act, well . . .

There may also be a few suggestions that you disagree with. Again, that's the performer's right. Whoever is at the microphone decides.

As a writer, I've argued with many comedians about material. Sometimes I've argued vehemently. That doesn't mean I've always won or I've always been right. However, I did have my say.

Likewise, this book is my say. You may know enough to overrule some of the suggestions, or you may simply elect to ignore them. I would caution you, though, not to dismiss too many of them cavalierly. Read them, study them, think about them, perhaps even try them. Then if they don't work, toss them aside.

I was a young writer once and I had young writer's ideas. Some producers tactfully shunted them aside; other producers weren't so delicate. Later, when I got a little more power, I tried my ideas. They stunk.

Then I became a veteran writer, a producer. Young writers came to me with ambitious ideas. I tried to dissuade them, sometimes tactfully and sometimes not. Probably most of them didn't listen to me and learned their ideas didn't work the same way I did—the hard way.

Experience has taught me that it pays to listen to people who have been there. You don't have to heed all of their advice, but it is wise to hear it.

So read on with an open mind. Dissect the suggestions. Decide which are right, or which might be right for you. If a few of them are beneficial and you get to be a rich and famous comedian, and you find you need a writer . . .

Part One

Your Attitude

1
THE MAGIC BULLET

"Is there a magic bullet that can insure success?"
"Yes."
"Is it foolproof?"
"Absolutely."
"Is it easy?"
"That depends on you."
"Is it fast?"
"As fast-acting as it has to be."
"Well, can I have it?"
"Not yet."
"Why?"
"Because you'll appreciate it more and maybe remember it longer if you have to wait a few pages for it."
"Who cares, Big Shot? I can go to the bookstore and buy any one of hundreds of books that promise on the front and back covers to give me the secret to success."

That's true. There are numerous books on the shelves that offer the keys to success. However, they probably don't have what you want. It's not because the books are at fault; most people's expectations are unrealistic.

Let's review the above dialogue once more and see what people really want.

"Is there a magic bullet that can insure success?"

People want the best for themselves. They want fame, fortune, and comfort. That's good. That's the drive that gets us going. It's the reason why you picked up this book. It's why you want to be a recognized star in the world of stand-up comedy.

That desire is commendable and it's reasonable. It's the rest of the dialogue that becomes suspect.

"Is it foolproof?"

You see, people want a formula that has no risk. That's practically impossible. Even if such a book did exist at your local bookstore, there would be risk involved. You have to drive to the bookstore, and with the drivers on the road today, that's risk.

Taking the risk out of any accomplishment would also take most of the fun out of it. I've listened to old-time show-business stories from many of the legendary comedy performers—Lucille Ball, George Burns, Milton Berle, Danny Thomas, Alan King. They talk about the lean years, the struggles. They laugh and kid about the times they couldn't find work, or when they did get work, they flopped.

Why are these stories so precious to them? Because they make what they have today that much more valuable.

I once complained to a tennis professional who ran a tournament that he put me in a part of the tournament that was too tough for me. I said, "I can't win when I play in that section."

He said, "The purpose of this tournament is to have some fun, to play against some competition that is tough enough for you to enjoy."

I said, "No, I want to win."

The next year he put me in a section of the tournament with downright beginners. I could have beat most of these people playing with a ping-pong paddle. Playing in this bracket, though, was no fun and I couldn't take pride in any victory. I dropped out of the tournament.

The tennis pro was right. The purpose of competition is to force players to give their best. Only then can they fully enjoy both the challenge and the victory.

So you want to take on a challenge that has some risk to it. It's the only way you'll be forced to concentrate on your efforts and give your all. It's the only way you'll enjoy your success when you attain it.

"Is it easy?"

People expect a success formula that requires little effort. One comedian kidded those quick-success advertisements: "I can teach you to dance in ten easy lessons . . . or two really hard ones."

People want the formula to do all the work. They expect to pick up a book, or listen to a series of tapes, or attend a class, and then automatically become a comedy smash. It doesn't work that way and it shouldn't.

The cliché applies: "If it were easy, everybody would be doing it." If comedy were a snap, not only would the field be woefully overcrowded, but it would pay next to nothing. Things that are easy, that anybody can do, pay the minimum wage. Comedy is difficult; it pays considerably more.

Effort is what produces worthwhile results. Suppose you want to develop a beautiful, muscular, slim body. You sign up for several sessions a week at the gymnasium under expert tutelage. Your coach tells you to lift 100-pound weights, but you decide they weigh too much and make you break out in a sweat. You overrule the coach and decide to lift nothing heavier than two pounds. It's easy, but you'll be just as flabby after twenty weeks of your workout as you were when you first signed up.

The pain of comedy forces you to improve. If you step on stage and bomb, you're going to want to find out why.

Was it the material? Was it the delivery? Was it the audience? Whatever the cause, you don't want to do it again. If it was the material, you'll be sure to get better stuff for the future. If it was your performance, you'll change it, improve it. If it was the audience, you'll vow to study them more before performing, or never to work in places like that again.

On the other hand, if you never felt the anguish, you'd never feel the need to improve.

"Is it fast?"

Why does it have to be? There's a story told about a successful man who was not content with his life. He told an advisor, "I always wanted to be a doctor." The advisor said, "You've got the money and the time, sign up for medical school." The man said, "That would be silly. By the time I got out, I'd be fifty years old." The friend said, "That's right. And how old would you be at that time if you didn't go to medical school?"

If any success formula is fast, it's probably not worth much. Some things should take time. Would you want to be on the operating table when the surgeon said, "This is great. Last week I was a welder, but I took this course on Instant Surgery and here I am—operating on my first patient."

Fast jeopardizes any gains you do make. You occasionally hear experts say of a particular boxer, "They brought him up too fast." That means the guy had a few flashy wins, got a lot of publicity, fought against a seasoned pro, and got his nose rearranged. He hadn't seen enough good fighters to know how to handle a class boxer.

It's the years in development that make you ready for the big time when you arrive there. Get there too soon and you may be leaving just as quickly.

I once asked Bob Hope what made him Bob Hope.

What made him good enough to last in a competitive business as long as he had? He said, "It was the tab shows."

Tab shows were a form of vaudeville where a repertory company would do as many as seven shows a day. In those shows, the performers would often switch roles. One person might play the straightman one day and the comic the next. Hope said it was intensive training that prepared him well for his debut on Broadway.

Other performers asked why he wasn't real nervous on the opening night of his first Broadway show. He said, "I had opening nights seven days a week in the tab shows."

Robin Williams perfected his craft as a street performer in San Francisco. Jay Leno crisscrossed the country for years working small comedy clubs before he earned a starring spot on "The Tonight Show." It takes years to become an overnight success.

"Can I have it?"

When's the last time in your life you were ever handed anything for nothing? Sure, you can have it, but there is a price tag. It's not necessarily a monetary price tag, but a fee that has to be paid in effort, dedication, devotion, perseverance.

The magic bullet that insures success is: Be good. That's it—be good.

All of the self-improvement books list various formulas that you can explore. Some of them are reasonable; some are loony. Some may require that you recite certain aspirations repeatedly, read three times daily from a contract you make with yourself. A few may suggest meditation. Some of them offer a do-this-one-day-and-do-this-the-next-day formula. But all of them are trying different ways to get you to be good at what you want to do.

The bottom line is that you have to be good. How you get to be good is up to you. You can do it on your own through study and practice. You can select one of hundreds of books to give you direction or to speed up the process. That's fine, but eventually, you have to be good.

Why is being good so important?

Excellence can't be denied. If you're really good and keep getting better, you won't have to search out success—it'll find you.

Let's consider two tennis players. One isn't very good, but has an uncle who is very influential in the tennis world. The "hacker" arranges through his relative to play against some of the greatest tennis pros in the world. He's hoping that, by getting to know them, he'll get to Wimbledon and win that prestigious championship. How much of your hard-earned money would you bet on his chances?

The other is a slightly better tennis player than John McEnroe. However, he doesn't know anyone in the sport; he just plays on the public courts whenever he can. You know that he's going to play the best on those courts and annihilate his opponents. He's going to be talked about so much that better players and perhaps some coaches are going to come to watch him. They might even challenge him to play some accomplished players. If he's as good as I said, he'll beat them, too.

Someone will get this kid into tournaments and he'll win many of them. He'll get to Wimbledon and he'll have a good chance of winning.

These kinds of stories happen in the comedy world. Look at the meteoric rise of Robin Williams. He was a street performer in San Francisco, but he was so good that he was noticed by television producers, starred in "Mork and Mindy" and made that show a success, then went on from there.

Whoopi Goldberg was noticed quickly and went on to great success.

It's the story of many comics who have graduated

from the comedy-club circuit. They're good, they're professional, and success finds them.

There are no time constraints on being good; you can do it at your leisure, at your pace. One of the most frustrating aspects of auditioning, submitting written material, or even job hunting is that you have to wait until the decision makers get back to you. They take their time while you sit home biting your nails.

They cost you hours of anxiety and weeks of wasted time, then opt to pass on your talents. It can be infuriating.

To be good or to get better, you don't need to wait for anyone. You can study when you want, read anytime you choose, rehearse whenever you feel like it, watch other comics. You're the master of your own schedule.

Bernard Baruch, an advisor to presidents from Wilson to Kennedy, knew that he could use his own time schedule for self-improvement. At a press conference on his ninety-fifth birthday, he announced that one of his goals for the upcoming year was to learn to speak Greek fluently.

A reporter asked, "Mr. Baruch, you're ninety-five years old, why would you want to learn to speak Greek now?"

Baruch said, "Well, sir, it's now or never."

You are in total control of being good. Vic Braden, a well-known tennis coach, advises his students to develop an effective serve. He says, "It's the one shot in tennis in which you totally control the ball."

In developing your comedy technique—in being good—you're like the server in tennis. You're in control. You don't have a club owner saying, "Hey, you're only allowed to do four minutes." You don't have producers saying, "You're too loud." There are no audiences sitting in judgment of your material, deciding whether to laugh at this joke or that joke. There are no people telling you what to do or how to do it.

Eventually, of course, you'll be faced with that. When you audition, you'll be at the mercy of producers, directors, and club owners. For now, though, when you're developing your talents, you are the boss. You're the decision-maker.

How do you go about being good?

First, you have to be cold-bloodedly realistic in evaluating your own skills and performances. Comedians tend to rationalize their mediocre performances. They want to blame it on the writers, the audience, the lighting, the sound system, the day of the week, the grimness of the news broadcasts, the President or Vice-President of the United States, the weather, the ozone layer, their wives and children, or anything else at hand.

Sometimes the bad response is the fault of one of those variables, but often the performer's to blame.

In order to analyze one's own performance, in order to know what to do to be good, the entertainer first has to be honest about the performance.

What did you do that contributed to the mediocrity? What could you have done to make it better? Even if the problem was one of those in that list above, how could you have handled it better?

I've heard comics come off the stage at a comedy club and say, "I was the best comic on the bill. People just didn't laugh at me. They laughed at the other guys, but not at me."

One comic even complained about the other performers with tongue in cheek. He said, "The comedian before me was so bad that in the middle of my act, people decided to get up and walk out on him."

Only by being cold-bloodedly realistic can you spot where improvement is needed. I have worked with a few aspiring stand-up comedians who do the same act time and time again. Friends advise them to change the act. Yet they continue to do the same material. Each time it flops. Each time they insist that the material is funny but audiences refuse to realize it.

That's hard-headed nonsense. It's not the audience's fault; it's the comic's.

By refusing to see or recognize the truth and utilize it, these people pass up an opportunity to get better, to be good.

I asked Jay Leno once if he thought the comedy clubs were a good or bad influence on today's comics. He said for the smart ones they were good; for the others they were bad.

The smart young comedians listen, learn, and get better. The others never progress.

Vic Braden tells about tennis students who complain to him, "Vic, I've got ten years of playing experience, but I never seem to get any better." Braden says, "No. You've got one year of playing experience ten times."

If you don't recognize reality and see the truth, you'll never work to correct it.

Second, observe other performers. It's tough for comedians to admit that some other performer may be better, or more successful, than they are. Each performer thinks he or she is the best, if not the only, good comedian in the business.

But we all know that any good comic can capture an audience on a given night. When they do, rather than berate your own bad luck, or rationalize their good fortune away, you should study their performance. Why were they hot this night? What was different about their performance that captivated this audience? Was their material that good?

Learn from their good fortune rather than let it demoralize you.

Every so often, a performer will break out of the pack. It might be a person you've shared the stage with many times. You didn't think this particular comic was that inventive or brilliant, but somebody obviously did. Suddenly, this person is getting better gigs and higher pay. He or she is getting the rewards that you feel you deserve.

You may be right; life may be unfair. Rather than slump into a corner and feel sorry for yourself, it's better to investigate why they succeeded. What did they do that impressed the producers? What gimmick did they have that worked? What can you do to better your chances for being the next one to distance yourself from the also-rans?

Feeling sorry for yourself is fun, but it's not helping you to be good. What will help you be good is an awareness of your business. Know who is hot and who's not, and why. Catch every comic you can to learn what they're doing right and what they're doing wrong. Then apply that information to your own act.

Third, study your craft. There are books available, and there are teachers. Some are good and some are not so good. Some of their proposals may work for your comedy style; others may not. The only way you'll find out which is which is to investigate.

Some comics feel they jeopardize their unique style if they study someone else's techniques. There's minimal danger of that. The potential gain far outweighs any possible loss. You can study, analyze, and select. Pick out what works for you, or what might work for you, and discard the rest.

You can also learn from studying the old-timers of your profession. You may not particularly like the style of the comedians who have been around for years. You may feel that their material is old, tired, and not as hip as yours. Nevertheless, they have survived in a tough business for a long time. They have something to offer. If you're not a fan of their comedy style, you can still learn from their stage presence, their show-biz savvy, their marketing and promotional techniques.

Don't dismiss the older generation too quickly. They might be able to help you be good.

Fourth, experiment. Improvement implies change. No one, including you, can get better if he or she stays the same. Granted, some of the things you try may not work. That's no problem. You get rid of them and you're right back where you started. However, some of them may work.

I know that many nightclub comics are afraid to take a chance. Some ask me to write new, innovative, fresh material, then they are afraid to try it out onstage. Instead, they go with their sure-fire laugh-getters, even if it means that their act will stagnate over time.

Blue material is another good example of comics being afraid to experiment. The off-color joke usually gets a laugh, even if it's only a nervous laugh from the audience. Young comics know that they have to develop "straight" material if they want to land a spot on TV. They know they have to try out clean material, and break it in, if they want to impress producers and talent coordinators. Yet they won't take that chance.

Each time they step onstage, they revert to the naughty stuff. It gets a laugh, they feel secure, but they haven't gained anything, they haven't learned anything.

To be good, you have to take a risk. You have to try new, fresh material. Sometimes it will flop, and you might flop along with it. But over the long haul, you'll improve your act and your opportunities for advancement.

Fifth, you must practice and rehearse. As a television writer, the performer I used to dread most was the self-assured, "trust me" type of actor. They'd say, "Don't worry about the lines, just put me out there with a piece of business and I'll be funny. I'm a very funny physical comedian. Trust me."

We'd put them out there with a piece of shtick, and no solid lines or pre-arranged pieces of business, and we'd get an actor who died on stage and tried to blame the writers.

You have to rehearse. You have to know what you can and can't do, and how well you can do what you can do. You have to know your skills and your limitations.

You must create new material and try it out on audiences to sharpen it. You have to perfect your timing and delivery, develop your stage presence. Jay Leno once told me that beginning comedians should first learn to *speak* with confidence before they attempt to be funny. It all takes practice.

Being good is a continuing process.

The minute you think you're good enough, you ain't.

As soon as you get good, you'll want to get better. Why? Because your definition of "good" will always be changing. As soon as you reach one plateau, you'll want to attain another. I guarantee that once you get what you want, you won't be satisfied with it.

Let's suppose that you are a raw beginner. Your goal right now is to be good enough to get on an open-mike night at some comedy club. So you work toward that end. Finally, you do get good enough to be given a time slot. You do well.

Now you want to continue to do well enough so that you'll be invited to become a regularly scheduled comic at that club. You do.

That's still not enough. Now you want to be so good that you'll be able to travel the circuit, become a recognizable draw at comedy clubs around the country, and make a decent income from that.

Once you accomplish that, you won't be satisfied. Now you'll want to get so good that the television production companies will be impressed. They'll audition you, and perhaps offer you a spot on a national TV show.

Maybe you even get to headline the show. You still won't be satisfied. You'll want the ratings to be in the top ten. You'll harass the writers until they give you scripts that will guarantee ratings.

Maybe they do and you become a top TV star. You'll want to get movie offers.

Suppose you get the movie offers and you're a smash. You'll want to produce and direct your own shows.

That's just the way most show-business egos are constructed. It's a good thing they are, too, because that's what provides the drive that makes stars.

If you have that sort of drive, you're blessed. However, remember that the first step is to be good. Be good at what you're doing right now.

There are gimmicks, tricks, and deceptions that might get you a chance at the top. You can lie about your experience or sleep with the producer. Being good, though, is the easiest way to get where you're going, and it has the best prognosis for long-lasting results.

The people who survive are not the ones with a gimmick, or who tricked their way into success; they're the ones with honest-to-goodness talent.

2
IF YOU'RE GONNA DO IT, DO IT

Stand-up comedy requires a commitment, an aggressive commitment. When I watch my grandsons' soccer games on Saturday mornings, I'm amused by the wide spectrum of participation. The players are only eight to ten years old. Some of them know how soccer is played and some don't. Some of them care how the game is played; others don't. A few of them are fierce competitors who chase the ball all over the field. Others are content to confine themselves to a small area of the field. If the ball comes near them, they might make an attempt to kick it somewhere. Otherwise, they just watch their cohorts scampering about.

Stand-up comedy demands that you be one of the fierce competitors. I don't mean that you have to throw yourself into the fray like a crazed soccer player, trying to cripple anyone who gets in your way. But I do mean that you have to get involved. You have to get into it.

Performing stand-up comedy is like bungee jumping. You're not bungee jumping when you're standing on the edge of the platform looking down at the earth below. You're not participating while you're trying to screw up the courage to make the plunge. So long as you're teetering on the edge, you're only teetering on the edge. You may be suited up with protective gear. You may have all the equipment strapped on correctly. You may be able to converse with bungee jumpers about bungee jumping. But you're not a bungee jumper.

It's not until you dive off the platform, throw yourself into the hands of gravity, that you become a real jumper. You have to commit.

The first commitment, of course, is to get into the business—to actually do it. You must step out on a stage with your material and a microphone and face your audience.

It's not easy. Many of us find ways of avoiding that moment. When I first began in comedy, I tried to hide behind a partner. If I were going to fail miserably, I wanted either someone to blame or someone to share my agony. I was asked to do a skit at a retirement party for my supervisor at work, so I wrote some one-liners about him. Then I converted the one-liners to dialogue just so I could invite another person onstage with me.

The night of the presentation, my partner didn't show up. I quickly converted the dialogue back to a monologue and presented it alone. My knees were shaking, my voice was quaking, but I got before the microphone and performed.

That gave me the courage to continue doing monologues, and I never performed with a partner again. (Of course, I later found another way of avoiding performing. I became a writer.)

Some people can't do it; some won't do it. However, those of you who want to do it have to get out there and do it. You have to struggle to get on at open-mike night. You have to try to get agents, room owners, and bookers to put you up there. You have to face audiences and occasionally fail before them. You have to take the bumps and bruises the industry has to give. It's the only way you become a pro. It's the only way you get to be good.

However, there's another type of commitment that you as a stand-up comedian have to be aware of. That is the commitment that once you do get onstage, and anytime

you get onstage, you will give the goshdamnedest performance you have in you. You must pledge to give each
audience, whether they deserve it or not, every bit of skill,
moxie, and energy that you've got.

I mentioned earlier that I started in comedy by doing
presentations where I worked. At one event, I hired a
sound engineer to tape my performance. I was going to
make a comedy record and enjoy the same success that
Bob Newhart did. This night I wasn't a success. The jokes
bombed and I folded.

After the show, I asked the sound man if he would
do another show. I assured him that my talks usually went
over great and the audience loved my presentations. This
night was the exception, not the rule.

He turned me down flat and told me why in no un-
certain terms.

"You quit," he said.

"I didn't quit," I defended myself. "The audience
wasn't with me tonight. It was just a bad night."

He said, "Who's your idol in comedy?"

I said, "Bob Hope."

"If Bob Hope was having a rough time, do you think
he'd just give up or would he work harder to win the
crowd over?"

I said, "I guess he'd work harder. But after all, he's Bob
Hope."

The engineer said, "That's how he got to be Bob
Hope—by working harder when the going got tough."

He was right. My first few jokes didn't work and I totally surrendered.

A few years later I was writing for comedian Slappy
White. He invited me to go to the Latin Casino with him
to see Liberace. I wasn't a big Liberace fan, but Slappy
talked me into seeing his act.

"If you want to be in show business, you gotta learn
about show business."

So I went.

What an education. Liberace came on stage and captivated that huge audience. The Latin Casino in New Jersey could hold an audience of over 2,000 and Liberace packed them in. It felt like he just threw a huge lasso around the entire crowd and then slowly started pulling the loop tighter and tighter until he had the entire audience right where he wanted them.

Liberace never was a great musician. He couldn't sing, he couldn't dance, he wasn't a comedian. He was, though, a showman who worked with great energy and enthusiasm. His passion seduced his audience.

I've been backstage with Bob Hope when he was exhausted from the travels of doing the military shows under wearying conditions. Yet when his theme music began and the emcee called him on stage, he'd stand tall and erect and bounce onto the stage. He summoned his energy because the performance demanded it.

I've watched great entertainers like Sammy Davis, Elvis Presley, Dean Martin work and they always stand there as if they own the stage. Today's comedians like Whoopi Goldberg, Robin Williams, Billy Crystal, and Jay Leno perform with unremitting confidence. Their bearing says, "I'm on this stage because I deserve to be here and you folks are going to listen to me and be entertained."

That's showmanship. That's being a solid trouper.

Showmanship is different from being talented. It's being confident. You can appear before an audience with a minimum of talent and *sell*. You might even enjoy some success that way.

However, it's almost impossible, even with considerable talent, to be successful if you don't present yourself with confidence.

I've watched many aspiring stand-up comedians at open-mike nights, workshops, and seminars doing their routines. One of the most common faults I see is that they back away from their routines and from the audience. They're timid. They're not sure they're good enough and so they hold back. Their delivery is halting and unsure. They want audience acceptance, then presumably they'll break out and present themselves with gusto.

It doesn't work that way. You must step onstage as if you belong there, as if you were born there. When you take the stage and grab the microphone, you have to be in charge—of the room, of the audience, and of yourself.

You may be terrible. Your material may be amateurish. I don't care. You still have to project confidence. You still have to stand onstage as if it's your birthright. The spotlight is on you and it's your responsibility to convince all viewers that that's exactly where it should be.

"Wait a minute, though," a few of you may say. "If both me and my material stink, why do I want to come on with that much arrogance? If I'm that bad, shouldn't I hold back a little so I don't get damaged too badly?"

No. And here's why:

When your stage demeanor is strong and confident, you give your best performance.

You'll deliver the maximum you have within you. Those of you who have ever tried any sport know this. When you're afraid to swing at the golf ball, that's when you make your most inept shots. You don't want to hit the ball quite as boldly as you should because you might hit it too far, too short, or in the wrong direction. Consequently, you hold something back and you wind up hitting the ball too far, too short, or in the wrong direction. The same happens in tennis. When I hit my overheads firmly, they go fairly well. When I say to myself, "Oh boy, I might miss this shot, so I'd better hit it more carefully," I miss it.

It's true of almost everything. In pouring liquid from a too-full container, if you make a decisive move, the fluid flows nicely into the glass. Pour tentatively, though, and the liquid dribbles down the outside of the container and makes a mess. When you hold back out of fear, you take something from your performance.

Be bold, aggressive, and you work to your peak. Now understand, your skills may still be lacking. You may still be bad, but you'll be the best "bad" you're capable of being.

When I hit a tennis shot confidently, I hit it about as well as I can hit it. That doesn't mean that I've become a John McEnroe. No way. I still play like me, but I play like a better me than when I play timidly.

So not having a strong comedy act doesn't excuse you from entertaining with enthusiasm and confidence. Not having experience is no reason for not being powerful onstage.

Only by performing to your fullest capabilities can you evaluate your performance.

I confessed earlier to selling out to an audience when my first few jokes failed. I quit. Oh, I finished the routine, but with no fervor. I simply recited the lines as meekly as I could so as not to draw much attention to myself. I ran through my jokes fast so that I could get off the stage as quickly as possible. I didn't sell any of my material.

Consequently, I don't know if any of that later stuff might have caught on. Certainly no one was going to laugh at it the way I was delivering it. Had I worked harder, as the sound engineer said I should, would I have turned the audience around? I don't know. I'll never know.

Becoming a successful stand-up comic is a process of learning. Which jokes are working? Which jokes do I do well? Which do I do badly? How should I move about the stage? You'll never learn the answer to these and other pertinent questions if you don't go full out. If your performance is in question, none of the input you get is valid. It's all tainted by your lackluster showing.

Sometimes a magnificent performance can redeem substandard material, but brilliant material will hardly ever salvage a weak performance. It's like the actor who was appearing in one of Shakespeare's plays, and doing badly. So badly, in fact, that the audience booed. He stepped to the footlights and said, "Don't blame me, folks. I don't write this crap."

If you throw yourself at your audience with confidence and gusto, if you do your material just as well as you possibly can, and they still don't laugh—then you might have to re-evaluate your performance . . . or your material . . . or both.

That's not a bad thing, though. A bad show in comedy is not catastrophic. Not learning why you were bad is far more harmful. And unless you give at least 100 percent of yourself, you can't learn from your performance.

So work as hard as you can. Your delivery may need some fine tuning, your material may need some polishing, the pacing of your act may have to be reworked. But try never to come off the stage with the feeling that your enthusiasm was the culprit.

Your confidence may relieve the audience's stress.

You've been in the audience. You know it's awkward, downright uncomfortable, to sit there and watch a comedy performer "die." The people sit there and they feel bad. They feel pity. Pity is the worst atmosphere to have pervade a comedy room.

Your bravado, your powerful presence, reassures them. They feel they're in the hands of a professional. That gets them on your side.

How would you feel if you went to a dentist and he sat you in the chair, put the bib around your neck, tilted you to the right position, adjusted the lamp, turned on the drill, and then said, "Gee, I don't know if I really should be doing this. I mean, I know how and all—after all, I did pass it in school—but I just don't want to screw it up, you know. Maybe I'll just drill a small hole in your tooth first to see how I do, you know. Then if that goes well, I'll drill the rest of it and then fill the cavity. Maybe that would be the best thing to do."

You'd be out of your chair and in your car in no time.

Would you fly on a plane where they had to plead with the pilot to get into the cockpit. "C'mon, Captain Wilson, you can fly the plane. You've done it hundreds of times before. Don't be afraid. You can do it."

No way would you sit there and fasten your seat belt.

Neither can you expect an audience to relax and enjoy your act when you're reluctant. They sense your lack of confidence and it affects their reaction to you.

If you don't go onstage strong, you won't allow them to enjoy you. They can't—anymore than you could enjoy letting that dentist work on your teeth or flying with that pilot.

Your confidence may sometimes be the only thing needed to guarantee your success.

Entertainers call this attitude "selling." That's exactly what it is. It's convincing people that your product is good. It's persuading an audience to like what you're doing for them.

I don't pretend to know much about music, but I do know that I've enjoyed performances simply because the musician convinced me that I was having fun listening to him. I once sat in at a rehearsal where the late Jim Croce strummed his guitar and sang "Bad, Bad Leroy Brown." He had the entire roomful of jaded stagehands and cynical writers clapping their hands and stomping their feet, even singing along. He made the song come alive with his vibrant energy.

Did he play the guitar well? Was he an accomplished singer? I don't know. I just had fun listening. That's what entertainment is about.

Too many of us hope the audience enjoys us. Our zeal should be telling them that they have to like us.

I learned by accident how the performer can control the audience. I was emceeing a benefit for a local church. We were doing two shows a night for several successive nights.

I told one joke that the audience laughed heartily at. I stepped away from the microphone to be sure that I didn't step on my own laugh. When I stepped back to the microphone, I got something caught in my throat. I covered my mouth and stepped aside.

The audience, though, thought I was laughing at my own joke, that it was so funny that it broke me up again. They laughed louder and they applauded. A friend said to me after the show, "You got applause on that one joke tonight."

I said, "I'm going to get applause on that joke at every show from now on." And I did. When the laughter died down, I pretended that it just struck me funny again. I turned away and laughed. Each audience laughed louder and applauded when I did.

It taught me that the entertainer doesn't have to rely on the audience to approve or disapprove, to laugh or not laugh. A confident—okay, cocky—performer can "sell." He or she can convince an audience—can tell the listeners—not in words so much as through stage presence and delivery, "I'm good, and if you don't believe it, that's your fault."

How do you develop this confident stage presence?

Begin simply by being aware of this phenomenon. Know and understand the principle that the more resolute your performance, the better the results will be. Some apparent exceptions may occur to you—Don Knotts as the nervous deputy of "Mayberry R.F.D." or Rita Rudner, who seems a quiet, shy performer onstage. Perhaps even

Steven Wright, who sheepishly turns away from his audience and delivers his wonderfully witty and inventive lines reluctantly. This, though, is their stage persona. It's the role they play, but they play it powerfully, confidently, and with inner resolve.

Preparation is a large part of confidence. You'll be more sure of yourself onstage when you're sure of yourself before you step onto the stage. There's a story about Bobby Darin beginning his nightclub act when someone from the audience shouted, "Bobby, you better be terrific."

Darin said, "Sir, you don't have to tell me that. I spend a half hour in my dressing room before every show telling myself the same thing."

Preparation includes selecting top-notch material and having that material ready. It means rehearsing so that you can deliver that material flawlessly. It includes your appearance, your wardrobe, your props. In short, it means doing everything you possibly can to make sure that you're as good as you can be when you step into the spotlight.

Finally, confidence implies a solid belief in yourself. You have a right to be onstage. You're entitled to pursue your dream of being a top-notch stand-up comedian. You're good. You may not have reached your apex yet, but you're getting there. You're learning and growing. You're good and getting better. When you honestly believe in yourself and your potential, you can do your best.

John Wooden coached the UCLA basketball team to many years of glory. He has a winning record that is unparalleled in college sports. Yet, Wooden never once mentioned "winning" to his student athletes. He stressed practice and preparation. On game night, he admonished them to *do their best.* That's the most he ever asked of his players. And it worked.

Each time you appear before an audience, you should resolve to *do your best.*

3
RESPECT YOUR AUDIENCE

Remember the "Late Night Television Wars?" The controversy raging over late-night television in the early 1990s? David Letterman demanded that NBC give him the 11:30 time slot or he'd bolt to another network. CBS had already offered him $16 million, which NBC had the contractual right to equal or top. Jay Leno, who was hosting the 11:30 time slot on NBC, said that if the network removed him from the 11:30 time slot, he'd leave. His contract was for that time slot; consequently, if NBC took it away from him, they would have to pay him off and release him. Supposedly, he would then have gone to CBS.

Both of the performers were assured of multi-million-dollar payments from someone. NBC had a predicament. Should they keep Leno and run the risk of Letterman going to CBS and stealing some of their audience? Or should they hire Letterman and face the threat of Leno going to another network and taking his viewers away from NBC?

Were the network executives, though, evaluating Letterman's talents against Leno's? Were they considering which performer was more charming? Were they asking themselves: "Is Jay funnier than David or is David more amusing than Jay?" No. They were asking themselves which of these two nighttime hosts would deliver the larger audience. Which one would attract the higher Nielsen ratings? Which of these performers would capture more people?

To make it in the entertainment industry you have to have an audience, a loyal audience, an audience that likes what you do.

Comedy is especially difficult to define, to explain. What is funny? Is a strong one-liner from Joan Rivers or Gary Shandling funny? Or is a goofy face and gesture from Judy Tenuta funnier? Is Mort Sahl's calm approach to humor more entertaining than Richard Lewis's zaniness? Are Lily Tomlin's characters funnier than Whoopi Goldberg's? What is funny?

As a writer, I've had to deliver "funny" lines to Bob Hope and Phyllis Diller. I've had to write funny sight gags for Carol Burnett, Harvey Korman, and Tim Conway in their sketches. I've had to construct wacky premises for the performers on "Three's Company" and "Welcome Back, Kotter." How did I know what was funny and what wasn't?

I didn't. Nobody knows. All we do is make educated guesses. We take the basic material, rehearse it, polish it, perfect it, then we perform it in front of an audience. If they laugh, it's funny; if they don't, it needs more work.

What's funny is what makes people laugh. As a stand-up comic, you're dependent on those people out front.

Comedy has grown tremendously in these past several years. Comedy clubs flourish in every city, and young hopefuls struggle to make open-mike night. Every area has aspiring comics, regulars, and headliners. They form a sort of brotherhood and sisterhood of comedy.

Many of them, though, treat this as a secret society. They turn it into an "us against them" thing. We're hip; they're not. They almost exclude the "outsiders" who sit in their audiences. They look down on them, almost dislike them.

This is wrong. No one has become a national success in comedy by appealing exclusively to other comics. It may help get you bookings and help get you noticed. For years, I heard people in comedy say, "You've got to catch Jay Leno's act. He's the best in our business." But Jay Leno didn't make millions until he appealed to the vast audience that watches television. If they didn't like him, he would have been gone.

When you step onto a stage and stand behind a microphone, there is no fraternity, no sorority. It's you and your audience. They laugh at your jokes or they don't. They like you or they don't. They don't care whether your peers appreciate your jokes or not. They don't care if you dress hip, walk hip, or talk hip. They care about being entertained, and you're the person at the mike who is supposed to entertain them. If you do, they'll laugh and applaud. They'll make you rich and famous. If you don't, they'll say, "Bring on the next comic."

Success in comedy almost demands a likability. People can dislike a musician's personality, but dig the beat. They can disagree with a singer's politics, but enjoy the vocalizing. However, people have to like a comic to laugh at him or her.

I've heard statements like: "I don't think Roseanne Arnold is very funny." I'd ask why. "She's too whiney." Because her voice sometimes has a complaining edge to it, they reject her routines as unfunny.

Years ago, Shelley Berman built a successful career from some very funny recordings. It was a time when comedy albums were hot. Allan Sherman did song parodies. Vaughan Meader had a top-selling album that kidded the John Kennedy presidency. Bob Newhart first gained national prominence with his "Button-Down Mind" albums.

However, Shelley Berman appeared in a nationally televised show, a semi-documentary that went backstage during one of his appearances. They showed him onstage when a backstage telephone rang during a dramatic moment in his performance. Then they showed him throwing a tantrum backstage. He ripped the phone off the wall and threw it across the room. He berated his co-star, who placed the call.

It showed Berman in a very unfavorable mood. Some people disliked him after that and his career suffered. He never quite regathered the momentum he had before that show aired.

If people don't like a comic, they find it more difficult to laugh.

Some of you may be saying, "Wait a minute. There have been many successful comics who are antagonistic to their audience." That's true. Don Rickles is vicious . . . and successful. The late Sam Kinison was a respected comic who could be loud and belligerent. Bobcat Goldthwait can be pretty aggressive onstage.

An act doesn't have to be sycophantic to be successful. You don't have to genuflect to the paying customers. Nor must you change your style or your material to suit them. You can be aggressive if that's your comedy style. You can be fierce in pointing out the lunacy of some of our social beliefs. You can attack the Democrats or the Republicans, whichever you wish. Whatever your style, though, it must reflect a respect and appreciation for your listeners.

It's an attitude thing. People sitting out front know that Rickles is kidding. They knew that Jack E. Leonard was a likable guy whose shtick was being insulting. Danny DeVito's character on "Taxi" was a hit because he was so relentlessly evil that he was likable.

Audiences sense your attitude, your sincerity. They intuitively know how you feel about them. If you have a respect for each audience, that will work for you regardless of the type of material you use.

George Burns once said that you have to have sincerity to make it in show business. "If you can learn to fake that," he said, "you've got it made."

Someone once asked Will Rogers, who was a great commentator on the political and social scene, how he could attack so many powerful figures and get away with it. Rogers said, "If there's no malice in your heart, there can't be none in your jokes."

Some idealistic young comics might rebel. "I'm not going to be a sycophantic simpleton who slobbers over the spectators simply to gain celebrity status and wealth." It's not that at all. It's not softening your style or lowering your standards. It's teamwork.

Stand-up comedy is teamwork. It's an exchange between the comedian and the listeners. You give to your audience and you get from your audience. They get from you and they give to you. It's a necessary collaboration for several reasons.

Your audience dictates your timing.

Timing, most people agree, is the essence of good comedy delivery. Timing can sometimes make a weak joke seem strong and a strong joke seem stronger. But what is timing? It's a comic picking up subtle hints from the audience. It's not only reacting to your listeners' responses, but almost predicting them. It's like reading the minds of the crowd.

I compare a good punch line to pulling the rug out from under someone. There are many variables involved. You have to get the victim to stand on the rug in the first place. If you snatch it away and they're not standing on it, it's wasted effort. So, in comedy, you have to set up your audience.

Then you must swipe the rug away at precisely the right moment. If you're too early, they won't be on the rug; if you're too late, they'll have warning enough to jump off. There will be no surprise. Knowing when to tug that rug is timing. You have to know each audience to do that properly.

Here's an example. In my banquet speech, I tell a joke about writing for Phyllis Diller. Phyllis was injured and had to wear an upper-body cast for her opening in Las Vegas. She asked me to do an opening line that would explain the cast and dismiss it so that she could proceed with her regular act as written. So I tell my audience:

> When Phyllis walked onstage in Las Vegas, people were surprised to see this cast. Phyllis began by saying, "Ladies and gentlemen, I'd like to explain away this cast and also make a public-service announcement. If there are any people in the audience who have just bought the new book *The Joy of Sex* . . . "

I pause here because this usually gets a laugh. The word "sex" triggers a laugh, or the people are jumping ahead of me and writing their own punch lines . . . whatever. Then I add:

"There's a misprint on page 205."

This is the topper that gets the bigger laugh.

However, each audience reacts differently. Sometimes there's only a small laugh at the mention of the book title. Other times, the laughter is strong enough to make that the punch line. Sometimes I'll pause only slightly between the phrases. Other times, I'll milk it. I'll make the audience wait for the topper. It's only by reading and being attuned to the audience's response that I can judge when to deliver the last part of the line.

I'm sure you have lines like this in your routine. Each punch line, really, requires this sort of subtle timing. It requires listening to your audience.

The audience is an essential partner for your timing. When Bob Hope began his radio show back in the 1930s, the network offered an empty studio, no audience. When Hope asked where the people were, they said no audience was required. This was radio. They had machines that could provide the laughter. What did he need an audience for?

They were executives; Bob Hope was a comic. He knew he needed an audience for legitimate laughter, for laughter that was necessary for his masterful timing.

Edgar Bergen and Charlie McCarthy were broadcasting immediately before Hope's show in a nearby studio. Hope marshalled the pages to help him shanghai an audience.

They rearranged the ropes at the exit of Bergen's studio, rerouting all the people right into Bob Hope's studio. As they entered, Bob Hope was onstage welcoming them. "I'm Bob Hope and we're beginning a new radio broadcast this evening. We'd like to welcome you to be a part of it. We think you'll enjoy the show."

The theme music came up, Hope began his radio monologue with a live audience. The show, later converted to television, has been running successfully ever since. Hope has always had a live audience for his stand-up monologue.

Your audience is a partner in your performance.

A smart stand-up comedian recognizes the synergism of comic and audience, and utilizes it. A bright performer welcomes the audience into the act, not necessarily by asking for their verbal responses or by audience participation, but by making their reactions part of the comedy timing, by delivering the punch lines when they're ready for them.

I've seen many inexperienced comics effectively ignore the audience. They come onstage with a well-written, well-prepared comedy set, and they deliver it the way they rehearsed it, regardless of what the audience does.

The standard joke is the comic who has funny material berating his audience. He comes out, tells his first joke, gets a big laugh, and then says, "What is this . . . an audience or an oil painting? I know you're out there. I can hear you breathing." If they're laughing, why kid them about not laughing? This comic is not listening to the audience.

The other, possibly worse, example is the comic who delivers a little line that gets no laughs at all. Then she says, "Oh sure, you can laugh if you want to, but . . . " Why say, "you can laugh" when no one is laughing?

Your audience turns a good monologue into a dialogue.

Stand-up comedy is conversational. You walk onstage and you *chat* with an audience as if they're old friends. You tell them intimate things about yourself. Perhaps you even kid them about very personal things. It's chummy, friendly.

As a developing comic, you must learn to talk to your audience. Converse with them. You're not an automaton delivering an unalterable monologue like the statue of Lincoln at Disneyland. You're a live person talking to live people.

These live people react to your conversation, so you should notice their reactions. It enhances the conversation.

And you must respect the audience because they are an integral part of your performance.

Your audience can be an inspiration.

The audience also gives the performer a supernatural, metaphysical, emotional lift. They provide inspiration. They get into your head and make wonderful things happen.

I've seen performers ask their writing staff for a comeback line for a given set-up. We'd work for hours and never come up with a fitting line. Finally, the performer would go onstage, hear the audience responses, and come up with a perfect ad-lib.

Why could they sit with a group of creative, inventive people and not be able to think of a funny response, yet go onstage and instantaneously create the perfect line? It's that mystical boost that performers get from an audience.

That feedback adds some sparkle to your performance. You know from your own performing or from watching others onstage that you can almost see extra energy flow into an entertainer when the audience is responsive. You know from talking to performers backstage that when they come away from a particularly enthusiastic crowd they are almost on a high. They're uplifted. They have new spirit, renewed vitality. They feel they can conquer not only the world of show business, but the world.

Once when I was working on "The Carol Burnett Show" we had Telly Savalas as a guest. There was one particular sketch that he wasn't secure with. It involved him, Harvey Korman, and Tim Conway having a business lunch together. The dialogue was well-contructed double entendre. Although it all had to do with a client who had switched allegiance from one salesman to the other, it sounded as if it were a woman who had abandoned one lover for another.

Mr. Savalas didn't think that it was funny. Carol asked him to give it a try. At rehearsals, which were without an audience, Telly was less than enthusiastic. His performance was ordinary, at best.

On the night of the show, though, he delivered his first line and the audience laughed. You could see the transformation. First Telly looked out into the audience with a sort of stunned disbelief. Then a glaze of joy came into his eyes.

He delivered his next line with gusto, and a touch of ham. The enthusiasm and hamminess was exactly what we wanted in a zany variety-show sketch.

The audience pumped belief into Telly Savalas and brought some excitement to his performance. Because of it, he performed the rest of the sketch with the consummate acting skills he always possessed.

Your audience tells you what's funny.

Besides being an inspiration, the audience can also provide a measure of your effectiveness. If you pay attention to your listeners, they'll help you write your act. They'll tell you which parts are funny, which parts should go, and even which styles of comedy you do best.

I work with many aspiring comedy writers and performers. Often they ask, "Do you think this joke is funny?" What's the difference whether I do or not? More to the point, how reliable is my judgment?

Comics learn eventually that the audience tells them which jokes are funny. Every comedian has several jokes that he or she loves but that get nothing from an audience. So they have to go. They have to be relegated to the scrapbook. Or they're relegated to party stories. The writer will tell a group of people that he has a joke that he absolutely loves but he can't get an audience to laugh at. Then he tells the listeners the joke and they don't laugh.

At our Round Table convention each year, we have Mike Night. This is a pleasant cocktail party, dinner, and then stand-up comedy performed by some of our aspiring writers and performers.

One year, a young man asked several people to read his routine and evaluate it. All of us suggested cutting one piece of material. Nevertheless, he tried it out that evening at Mike Night. Most of his material worked well except for this one segment.

A few months later, he was performing at a local comedy club, and he invited me to be in the audience. He performed well, but finished his set with this same piece of material. It went over badly again.

I spoke to him after the show and mentioned that particular bit, suggesting once again that he cut it. He said, "Oh, I love that material and so does the audience."

He wasn't listening to his advisors. More importantly, he wasn't listening to the people. They didn't like this section of his act and it was tainting his entire performance.

When Bob Hope was doing his radio show live, he would bring an audience into his rehearsals and do an extra-long monologue. After the rehearsal, he and his staff would go over the script and check only those jokes that worked well. By listening to his audience, he would trim his monologue down so that the one he delivered live on the air would be sharp, full of only his best gags.

Good stand-up comedy must be fine-tuned. Generally, that means cutting out the weaker parts, trimming the fat. You can do that most effectively by listening to your audience response.

4
BE SOMEBODY

Recently I traveled with Bob Hope to San Antonio, Texas, to tape a Christmas show. While we were there, Bob Hope worked in the penguin display at Sea World. He was dressed as Santa Claus and he roamed about with all these little birds at his feet. It was a different look and turned out to be a cute sketch.

That evening, Bob Hope was doing a personal appearance, so he called me and asked for some material about working with the penguins. I came up with one line I was particularly proud of. Bob Hope said, "I did a show with the penguins today at Sea World. You know, penguins have wings but they can't fly. I know the feeling. I have golf clubs."

Forgive me for boasting, but technically it's a good line. It's based on fact. It has a surprise, which comes right at the end. It kids the comic and it's funny. I'm proud to have written it. However, I couldn't have written it if it weren't for the stage persona that Hope has built up over the years.

Bob Hope is a golfer. He has his own tournament in Palm Springs annually. He plays golf with presidents, statesmen, celebrities, and professional golfers. They kid him about his playing and he kids himself.

All of this background was part of writing that line. Would that same line have worked as well for Joan Rivers? Phyllis Diller? Rodney Dangerfield? Jerry Seinfeld? Obviously not.

The line was prompted by Bob Hope and his golfing identity. People know Hope plays golf, and they suspect that he probably plays badly. Had Joan Rivers, Phyllis Diller, Rodney Dangerfield, or Jerry Seinfeld worked among the penguins and asked me to write some lines about it, different ideas would have popped into my head. I would have taken a different approach.

Nevertheless, this line worked well for Bob Hope because he has created a strong characterization of the perennial amateur golfer.

Let me offer another illustration. Jack Benny was playing in a golf exhibition. He was putting on a pleasant show for the gallery gathered at the first tee. After a while, the tournament officials asked that the game begin. Jack Benny took out his golf club, turned to his caddy, and said, "Son, are you any good at finding lost golf balls?" The caddy proudly said, "Yes, Mr. Benny, I am." Jack said, "Well, find me one and let's get started."

It's a perfect gag for Jack because he developed an identity as the stingiest, cheapest man in the world.

So Hope's golf joke worked for Hope and Benny's golf joke worked for Benny. Would they work as well if you switched them? No. Benny created a comedy character for himself that was unique, peculiarly Jack Benny. And Bob Hope has his own persona that works best for him.

When an unknown, aspiring comic walks onstage, many people subconsciously ask, "Who the hell are you?" It's not a vicious thing. The people aren't being antagonistic. They just don't know who you are. You're job as a stand-up comic is to tell them "who the hell you are."

To do that, you have to know comedically, professionally, who you are and what you stand for. You have to know what you're going to talk about and what you're going to say about it. You must have a comic persona, a philosophy, a point of view. And it should be consistent.

Let me mention another joke that I think is technically perfect, tremendously effective, and which could only be done by one man. Jack Benny, on one of his radio shows, was trying to get himself invited to a big Hollywood party. He tried several devices, but none of them worked. Finally, he called his agent and ordered him to get him invited to the party. Over the phone, the agent said, "I can't do that, Jack. That's not my sort of work." Jack angrily replied, "Well, why can't you? Why am I paying you nine percent?"

Listeners laughed because they knew that only Jack Benny would be cheap enough to pay an agent only nine percent when the standard rate in show business was ten percent. No one else in radio could have gotten a laugh with that line. Not Bob Hope. Not Fibber McGee and Molly. Not Fred Allen. Not Edgar Bergen and Charlie McCarthy. None of them. Only Jack Benny.

That's what a strong comic characterization can do for a comic. It can make you unique, different, one of a kind. If I tell you I have a great one-liner about a guy who gets no respect, you know I'm talking about Rodney Dangerfield. How about a fantastic line about face-lifts? You'd guess it came from Phyllis Diller. If I mention a funny routine about power tools, you'd say it's from Tim Allen. If I mention a line that's hilarious but sounds like it was written by a Martian, you'd most likely be correct if you said it was from Steven Wright.

There's another benefit of having a powerful stage character—it helps make weak or ordinary jokes more powerful. Let me tell you about a gag that was supposedly the longest recorded laugh in show-business history. It was from radio, and again, it's a Jack Benny line.

In this scene, Jack Benny is walking along a street late at night. Suddenly, a mugger comes up behind him, holds a gun on him, and says, "Your money or your life." That got a laugh from the audience. It seems any connection of money with Jack Benny gets an anticipatory reaction from the listeners.

Then there was a long moment of silence, which got more laughs from the audience. They knew something was coming.

The mugger grew impatient and repeated his threat. "I said, 'Your money or your life.'" Jack Benny said, "I'm thinking it over."

It got screams of laughter from the audience, and supposedly the laughs continued for two minutes.

Technically, it's not that fantastic a line. In fact, it's hardly a constructed joke at all. But comedically, it was very effective because of the strength of Jack Benny's reputation as a tightwad.

Jokes are built on characterization. On "Cheers," Norm gets kidded about being heavy, out of work, and a voracious beer drinker. Cliff is boring, a Mama's boy, and hopeless with the ladies. Phyllis Diller's character is unattractive, a terrible housekeeper, and made up of spare body parts. Dangerfield gets no respect. Rickles is a vicious loudmouth who insults anyone within hearing range. Each successful comic has an identifiable stage persona. A well-defined characterization can help your career by providing you with a sort of a trademark.

It also helps your comedy by providing your listeners with a reference point. They know who you are and what to expect from you. You know that feeling you get when you're attending a classical concert and the music stops but you aren't sure whether you should applaud or not? When you're in church and you must look around to learn when to stand, kneel, or sit? That's the way an audience can feel with a comic. Is he serious about this or kidding? Is she man-crazy or a man hater? Does this comedian love his wife, tolerate her, or want to murder her? If the audience knows what your point of view is, they can more readily understand it and laugh at it.

Let me give you a rather extreme example of this. An unknown comic was playing the guitar and doing a few song parodies. Someone at ringside heckled. The comic responded with a putdown line. The ringsider heckled some more. The comic threw another insult line at him. The heckler said something else. The comic hit him over the head with the guitar.

The ringsider required stitches; the comic required a new guitar. The audience didn't know this comedian. They didn't realize that he didn't welcome asides from the audience as some comics do. When the barrage of insults began to fly from the audience to the stage and back, listeners weren't sure whether this was acceptable or not. Should they laugh at the heckler or shush him? Should they be amused by the performer's comebacks or be shocked by them? Naturally, when they saw the guitar splinter, they surmised that this particular performer didn't appreciate uninvited audience comments, especially unfriendly ones.

Without fixing any blame in this particular instance, it could have been avoided if the performer had defined his stage persona for this audience.

If they had known that this comic didn't want interruptions from the audience, the heckler might not have started the exchange. Or the audience might have quieted the offender before it reached the fighting point. Audiences are usually willing to go along with your act if they understand it. You have the obligation to tell them who you are, what you do, and what you think. You have to define your character for them.

A strong definition will also help you in creating your comedy. When you know who you are, what you do, and your point of view, the jokes will become more obvious to you. It's much easier to write jokes for a well-defined character. The character itself prompts ideas and gags.

Also, strangely enough, it's easier to ad-lib when you have a good idea of who you are onstage. Your frame of reference is focused more strongly, so the relationships and the jokes present themselves to your mind more readily.

You can test yourself on this. Imagine you're at an awards ceremony and the master of ceremonies is presenting an award to Bob Hope. As he hands him the trophy, the figure on the top of it falls off and clangs on the ground. What would Hope say?

Picture the same incident happening to Phyllis Diller? What would her comment be?

Can you imagine what Andrew Dice Clay would say?

Hope might relate this incident to his golf game. Phyllis would probably relate it to her body. And Andrew Dice Clay . . . well . . .

What would you say? What area would you compare this to? If you don't know, you should begin to find out.

The question now: How do you go about finding your effective stage persona? The answer is a combination of honest self-evaluation and trial and error. First you analyze yourself and your talents, then you try different things and assess the results. What works you keep; what doesn't work you replace.

These three questions will help you to analyze yourself:

1. What do you *want* to do?
2. What *can* you do?
3. What does the *audience* want you to do?

What do you *want* to do?

There are almost as many different styles of comedy as there are comedians. Jerry Lewis is different from Milton Berle who is different from Robin Williams who is different from Jay Leno who is different from Jerry Seinfeld who is different from anyone else you name. Joan Rivers is different from Roseanne Arnold who is different from Phyllis Diller who is different from Elayne Boosler who is different from Rita Rudner who is different from anyone else you name.

And there are different things to talk about for those

comedians. Tom Dreesen talks about his Catholic upbring-
ing in a tough section of Chicago. Gary Shandling talks
about his love life. Richard Pryor talks about the black
experience; Bill Cosby doesn't. Phyllis Diller talks about
herself and her family. Joan Rivers talks about people in
the news.

Even those comics who talk about the same topics do
it with a different technique, a different modus operandi.
Mort Sahl comments on the political scene; so does Jay
Leno, but they each do it completely unlike the other.

Many comics begin their careers by emulating people
they admire. Johnny Carson was unabashedly a disciple
of Jack Benny's. Woody Allen says that his film character
was fashioned after Bob Hope's. Robin Williams could be
a reincarnation of Jonathan Winters.

Other comedians come on the scene as one of a kind.
Steve Martin was unique. Lily Tomlin was fresh. Whoopi
Goldberg was original.

So you have some decisions to make. What are you
going to talk about? How will you present yourself? What
will be your comedic style? Will you take the technique
of a legendary performer and try to raise it to even greater
heights? Will you be a combination of two different performers? Dean Martin said of himself that he was Bing
Crosby's voice with Joe E. Lewis's tipsy shtick. Will you
create a new form of comedy?

How do you begin to answer these important questions? Where should you look for answers? You look to
yourself. What do you as a "civilian" like to talk about?
What are you interested in? What about you or your life
would be fascinating to an audience? If all you think about
is your love life, talk about your love life to your audience.
If you enjoy cars and gadgets, that might be the basis for
your humor. If you think of yourself as an egotist, talk like
an egomaniac. If you're insecure, be insecure onstage. If
you're quiet and reserved, you can be funny like Rita
Rudner. If you're brash and loud, you can be entertaining like Don Rickles.

Begin by talking about what you know. And do it in the way you normally talk. There's only one person in the world who can be you without any affectations. That's you. You play you better than anybody else in the world. So go with your strengths.

Remember, too, that if you create a character, you'll have to be that character for the rest of your professional life. It's not easy. You can tire very quickly of being someone you're not. So if you are going to manufacture a character, be sure you can tolerate that "person" for a long time.

Of course, there are comedians who have done well with characters. Lily Tomlin has been Ernestine, the telephone operator. She's been Edith Ann, the precocious child. Whoopi Goldberg also plays a number of different roles in her comedy act. That's the style of comedy that they chose, but they do come out of those characters eventually to be themselves, too.

Some comics stay in character throughout their professional lives. Harpo Marx was an eloquent, if silent, example.

My suggestion is to try to keep your stage persona as close to your own personality as possible. If you must become a character, chose it carefully. Woody Allen's comedy is largely a caricature, but it's one that Allen is comfortable with. It's close to his image of himself.

Think of some of the legends of comedy—people who you've admired and laughed at over the years. You'll most likely find that most of those are pretty much the same off-stage as they are on. Career longevity comes easier when you're comfortable with your own stage persona.

What *can* you do?

I worked on "The Carol Burnett Show" for five years, and people frequently commented to me how versatile they thought Carol Burnett was. She was. But she wasn't as versatile as people thought she was.

Carol wisely selected roles and played parts that she knew she could do. She appeared to be able to do everything well because she would only do those things she could do well. We even had sketches in which Carol would relinquish her role during rehearsal. She'd exchange parts with Vicki Lawrence or a guest star because that person could play the part better than Carol felt she could.

All good performers have this wisdom. Sinatra only sings songs that he feels suit his style and his range. Jugglers only do tricks they've mastered. High-wire walkers don't take chances up there. And the guy being shot out of a cannon wants to be reasonably sure that he's going to land in the net. That's just common-sense showmanship that applies equally as well to stand-up comedians.

Face it. There are certain things you do better than others. There are even some things you can't do at all. Everyone has limitations. Find out what your strengths are and then work within them.

I began my comedy career doing stand-up routines at banquets where I worked. I would do "roasts" for co-workers who were retiring or celebrating twenty-five years with the company. My routines were basically insult humor. I would write one-liners kidding the guest of honor.

People enjoyed them and asked me to emcee several of the parties that we had. No one took offense at my put-downs because I was a quiet, soft-spoken speaker who delivered barbs that were harmless.

Then at one banquet I decided to do a Don Rickles type of act. I attacked the guest of honor. The lines were basically the same as before, but they were delivered differently. I flopped. Why? Because I didn't have the personality to pull off such an aggressive type of humor.

When my lines were delivered in my normal reserved speaking voice, they were gentle. The audience and the guest of honor could laugh at them and enjoy them. When I delivered the same lines with what I thought was a Don Rickles type of mock ferocity, the audience didn't buy it. I couldn't pull it off.

I have seen people try to tell dialect jokes. Their Russian accent sounded exactly the same as their American Indian. I've listened to people do impressions where George Bush sounded similar to Richard Nixon. These comics didn't have sense enough to know that they were playing out of their league. They were attempting to entertain an audience with skills they didn't have.

There's nothing wrong with not having certain abilities. You and I may not be able to sing like Michael Bolton. What annoys an audience is when you and I think we can and insist on getting up onstage and trying to sing like Michael Bolton.

It's up to you, and it's for the good of your career, to honestly appraise your skills. Don't be afraid to take a chance and try something that stretches your talents, but having tried it be honest in critiquing your own performance. If you're not good enough, get better. If there's no way you're going to get better, don't do it anymore.

Do the things you do well, well. Those things you do badly—well, don't do them at all.

What does the *audience* want you to do?

Referring to "The Carol Burnett Show" again, we did a sketch for guest star, Roddy McDowell. In it he played a Pulitzer Prize-winning author who stopped by to visit his family on his way to England to do an interview with the Queen. He hadn't been home in some time. He was world-renowned, talented, and wealthy. The family, though, were more impressed with themselves and the tricks their dog had recently learned. It was a well-constructed, well-written, funny sketch.

The reason I mention it here is because that's all it was—a good sketch. However, the cast fell in love with their roles. They each played the hell out of them. And the audience fell in love with the characters. They laughed at Vicki Lawrence as an old lady and Carol Burnett as

Eunice, the frumpy homemaker. Harvey Korman played her beleaguered husband, Ed. Later, Tim Conway became Mickey Hart, Ed's assistant at the hardware store. These characters became regulars on the show, and later some of them spun off to a successful situation-comedy called "Mama's Family."

The "Eunice" series of sketches were probably the best remembered and enjoyed of all the sketches we ever did on Carol's show, with the possible exception of the *Gone With the Wind* takeoff.

Did the writers decide to create a group of characters who would score so strongly? No. We just wrote a sketch and the audience loved it. They were the ones who made it a repeating series of sketches.

Much of Dana Carvey's recent success is because he did an entertaining impersonation of President George Bush. He has done many different characters on "Saturday Night Live," but this one especially tickled America's funny bone.

Stephen Wright has a unique and successful comedy style. He speaks very softly, almost to himself rather than to the listeners. He also pauses often as though he's trying to remember what comes next. It works.

How did it evolve? Stephen Wright says that he speaks softly because he had terrific stage fright. He was unsure of himself when he first started to perform, so he spoke in a quiet, frightened voice. He acted as if he didn't really want the people out front to hear him. And he paused as if trying to remember his next line because he had a terrible memory. He was honestly trying to remember. The people loved it, though, and it has since become Wright's shtick.

The audience is the ultimate judge of your act, your style, and your material. They'll decide what's working and what isn't. You can guess, but they'll decide.

That's good, though, because it allows you to experiment. This is your opportunity to try different styles, varying approaches, fresh new bits and shtick. The audience is your gauge. They tell you which pieces they like coming from you.

You have to be smart enough to listen, and courageous enough to accept their judgment.

In literature, they say that a writer must find his or her voice. In entertainment, the stand-up comedian must find his or her persona. You have to find out who you are, what you want to say, and how you're going to say it.

Part Two

Your Material

5
GET GOOD MATERIAL

On one Bob Hope show, we had four military men with four stars, each representing a different branch of the service. There was General Westmoreland from the Army, Admiral Short from the Navy, General Wilson, who was former Commandant of the Marines, and General MacPeak, then Chief of Staff of the Air Force. I had to write material for them.

In order to make last-minute script changes, I interrupted a meeting of these men with Bob Hope and then Secretary of Defense, Dick Cheney. General Westmoreland wanted to make a few changes in his speech, so he asked me for a pen. I was embarrassed and had to tell him that I didn't have one.

As another General handed me a ball-point pen, Bob Hope spread his hands in resignation, turned to the gentlemen in the room, and said, "I have writers who don't carry pens."

You must remember those times in school when you forgot to bring a pen or a pencil. Your teacher said, "If you were a plumber, would you go to work without your wrench? If you're a fireman, would you forget your hose? If you were a mailman, would you leave your pouch home?" And the teacher was right. If you're a professional, you show up prepared. You bring with you the equipment you need to do your job effectively.

As a stand-up comedian, the equipment you need is material.

Earlier I mentioned the performer who said, "I'm a funny person. I don't need a script; just a basic outline." She pleaded, "Just give me something physical to do and I'll be hilarious. Have me dialing a phone and I'll turn it into classic comedy." She wasn't hilarious; she didn't do any classic comedy. Neither she nor the show survived long. It's very difficult to be funny when you're creating on the spur of the moment and off the top of your head like that. Few can do it. Many of those who think they can, can't.

We rarely allowed improvisation on television because so much of it is hit and miss. When it works, it's brilliant, but much of it doesn't work, and the television audience doesn't have the patience to wait. Also, when it works on television, it still doesn't work because the people suspect it's not pure improvisation, but scripted material. The impact of it is lost.

Besides, can you think of one time-tested, proven professional comedian who built his reputation totally on improvisation?

When comedy is performed well, it appears spontaneous—as if it just popped into that comic's head. It looks easy. Good material is designed to give the impression that this performer walked onstage and thought these jokes up as he or she went along. We writers noticed that when we did our job exceptionally well, no one knew we were even there. The better our jokes were, the more they seemed like extemporaneous bons mots.

Many years ago, I worked with a comic who was the opening act for Sammy Davis, Jr. From the back of the theatre, I watched Sammy do two shows a night for two weeks. In my anonymity, I could listen to the comments of the patrons as they exited the theatre. They'd say things like, "Boy, that Sammy Davis is amazing. I never knew he could ad-lib like that."

Yes, he ad-libbed. He ad-libbed the same lines at the same point in his performance, show after show, night after night. That was part of his brilliance as an entertainer, that he could appear completely spontaneous when the material was scripted, polished, and rehearsed.

Sammy went to the microphone prepared. His arrangements were orchestrated and rehearsed, his dance steps were choreographed. And he had his "ad-libs" ready.

Sometimes, entertainers can fool you. Even the ones you think are truly improvisational have their material prepared. I've worked several times with Jonathan Winters, one of the fastest and most creative minds in comedy. At a pre-production meeting, he began to tell a group of us some story about his relatives back home. He had us in stitches. We were amazed how he could sit in a room and come up with such hilarious anecdotes so quickly, so effortlessly.

Later, I saw Jonathan talking to several people backstage. He was telling the same story, with the same voice inflections, same jokes, same punch lines.

He told this same tale several different times to different people, but always the same way.

I've watched Robin Williams, whom some call a "comedy savant," and noticed that he'll repeat lines and bits from previous performances.

This is not to demean Jonathan's or Robin's creativity. They are lightning-fast comedy creators, and much of what they do is truly improvisational—and brilliant. However, they also have reliable material that they know will get laughs. And they use it to entertain.

Comedians need materia—tight, polished, professional, funny material. People often ask me: "What's the difference between Charlie, the guy who is funny around the office and at all the parties, and the comedian who gets up onstage and makes us laugh?" The difference is the discipline, the preparation, the material.

Being at a party with Charlie is not the same as paying $25 to sit in a club and hear Charlie speak at the microphone.

Charlie might be a genuinely creative and funny guy, but as a professional stand-up he has to bring a prepared act to the stage. He has to have jokes to stand with him behind the microphone. He has to know that he's going to get laughs, and he has to get them in fairly rapid succession. A paying audience is not going to wait for inspiration to strike Charlie. They're forking over money to have Charlie make them laugh. He'd better do it.

Material, then, is what separates you from the neophyte. Understand that comedy material is not the only thing a stand-up comic needs. Performers need poise, style, projection, stage presence . . . a lot of things to guarantee their success. Material, though, is essential.

A gunfighter needs courage, steady nerves, quick reflexes, sharp eyesight. Even with all those attributes, though, at the moment of truth, when he reaches for his Colt .45, if it's not there, he won't be in the business long. He needs all these other things, but he'd better bring a gun with him.

A stand-up comic better bring a few jokes, too. When you stand behind the mike and slap leather, you'd better have a few punch lines in your holster.

One benefit of good, solid, funny material is that it will make you stand out from the rest. Comedy, especially today, is a competitive and crowded field. Steve Allen once told me that comedy today is like rock and roll was in the '50s and '60s. "Back then," he said, "every kid had a guitar. Nowadays, every kid has six minutes that he can do at the comedy club."

It's not an occupation in which you can patiently wait until your turn for success comes. Big breaks are not handed out in the comedy profession on the basis of seniority. Advancement in comedy is meted out strictly on merit. If you're good and get noticed, you'll move ahead. If you're just one of the pack, you'll stay in the pack.

That crowded field, though, can be an advantage to you. How? Well, it promotes mediocrity. It makes room for a lot of people who are content to be just good enough. It creates a background against which the truly hard working and talented are clearly visible.

Let me try to explain what I mean by that. Take the National Basketball Association. There are twenty-seven professional teams in that league. That means there are roughly 324 players in the NBA.

A handful of those players are superstars. Certainly, Michael Jordan of the Chicago Bulls and David Robinson of the San Antonio Spurs are. But many of the players are journeymen, and a few are barely skilled enough to remain in the league.

Consider, though, if there were only three teams in the professional ranks. Then there would only be about thirty to thirty-six players. Only the best would survive. Michael Jordan and David Robinson would always be playing against the most skilled players, and only the most skilled. They would still be as talented and as gifted, but they wouldn't stand out as much as they do now.

So the more people there are in the field, the easier it is for the truly superior to stand out.

I've recently had two editors approach me and ask me to have writers I work with submit comedy material for their publications. Both said they desperately needed good humor submissions.

I was confused. Both of these were large, well-known publications. I said, "I've always heard that you were bombarded with thousands of submissions daily." They said, "We are. But most of it is average at best and bad at worst. Anyone who understands humor and can get funny material on paper will impress our editors immediately."

Talented humorists stand out because of the number

of average humorists who submit. The quality of the competition helps you look good.

If you step up to open-mike night with quality material, you're going to be noticed. Perhaps only by a few at
first, but eventually more and more will notice, and that's
how you find opportunity in the comedy business.

But where and how do you get quality material? You
have three choices:

1. You can research it.
2. You can buy it.
3. You can write your own.

Actually, I should add a fourth choice, which would
be a combination of all three.

Research it.

Research doesn't mean lifting other comedians' stuff. I
remember one comedian telling me a sad story about a
successful comic friend of his who took seriously ill. This
gentleman told me he called his friend and said, "I'm sorry
to hear about your illness. I wanted to be the first to call
and ask how you're doing and what you plan to do with
your material after you're gone."

Research, though, can mean reading joke books and
studying comedy. Becoming familiar with material that is
worthwhile. There are at least three benefits to this.

First, you begin to absorb the quality of this material.
Then, even though you may not duplicate the individual
jokes, you begin to duplicate their quality.

*Second, these jokes may springboard your mind to
similar jokes.* For example, when Bill Clinton and Al Gore
were about to be sworn in as President and Vice-President,
comedy writers were wondering what to write about Al
Gore. Then a few comics did jokes about how stiff Gore
was. Mark Russell did a song parody about him. Instead
of singing, as the Tin Man did in *The Wizard of Oz*, "If I

Only Had a Heart," Mark Russell had Al Gore singing, "If Only I Could Bend." Now all of us are commenting on how stiff Al Gore appears.

Third, you can always use some of the good jokes and do switches on them. For instance, there's an old joke about a Hollywood agent who was so cheap that he had his pockets made of oilcloth so he could steal soup. The oilcloth reference dates that joke, but you might change it to a friend of yours who is so cheap that he's had the trunk of his car converted to a doggie bag.

And again as an afterthought, I'll add a fourth category. Some jokes you may "steal"—from comics or humorists who are long past complaining of your plagiarism. The gags may be so old and so long gone and so buried in the archives that they're worth resurrecting. Many times in my research I've come across gags that were written in the 16th century and are being used by national comedians today. To me, that's valid research.

I asked Bob Hope how he got started as a comedian. He told me it was from jokes that he had heard. He'd always be on the lookout for new gags when he was playing vaudeville. He'd ask traveling acts if they had any jokes they could spare. That was how he initially built up his repertoire.

Buy it.

Buying material might seem to be the easiest method, but it isn't always. First, you need money (comedy writers are funny that way). Second, you have to get someone who can write solid stuff for *you.* You want funny, inventive, creative comedy. The gag writer wants money. The two goals are not always compatible.

Then again, you may find some writer who understands your style of comedy and can write it. What a formidable combination that is. Cherish it and exploit it.

A few chapters from now, we'll discuss the pros and

cons of working with comedy writers. For now, I'll just mention that it is a viable method of getting fresh, funny material.

Write it.

You can write your own comedy material. You certainly can't quarrel with the price. It may take time, study, effort, and practice, but then doesn't anything that's worthwhile?

You should be able to do it because basically it takes a sense of humor coupled with some common sense. If you want to be a stand-up comedian, you must have a sense of humor. You must enjoy and appreciate humor. You should be able to translate that to a facility for writing humor.

The techniques and skills of creating comedy are beyond the scope of this book. However, for those who are interested in writing their own routines, I'll unashamedly recommend two other books that I've written. The first is *Comedy Writing Step by Step* (Samuel French Trade, Hollywood, CA), which outlines the writing process to create jokes and routine them into complete monologues. The other is *Comedy Writing Workbook* (Sterling Publishing Co., New York, NY), which contains about ninety writing exercises to develop skills needed to write comedy.

Your material should be funny.

Regardless of how you get your material, it should have certain qualities. One would seem obvious, but when you watch and listen to some young comedians, you doubt it. The material should be funny.

I don't say that cynically and I don't mean to put down the beginning comics. I'm speaking more in a technical sense. The material you do onstage should have a payoff, a punch line.

I've watched a few comedians go into a long, drawn-out buildup, and then suddenly switch to their next topic. I'd say to myself, "Are you done with that? Did you open up this discussion just to end with that weak line?"

In other words, I got the feeling that they were building to a punch line, but what I thought was part of the buildup *was* the punch line. It was a letdown. As part of the audience, I felt disappointed, even cheated. As Shakespeare said, "Much Ado About Nothing."

Not each of your jokes has to be dynamite, but each section should at least have a potential payoff. As Bob Hope says when we review material, "Where's the biggie?" Where's the joke that makes talking about this subject worthwhile? If there is none, then we drop the topic.

When I would lose a schoolyard fight as a child, my Dad would remind me, "Don't start anything you can't finish." I'll offer the same advice to stand-up comics. Don't start any routine that doesn't have a payoff.

Your material should be worth the investment.

Comedy is like economics—each item has a price tag. I'm sure you like ice cream and you'd enjoy a double-dip cone right now. However, you wouldn't want it if I told you the price was $33,000. If it were a buck, though, you might buy it.

That's the way audiences are with punch lines. They'll accept some if you don't take too long with them, but if you spend a lot of time in buildup, the payoff had better be there.

When I worked on "Laugh-In," we could get away with some pretty hokey one-liners and sketches because they were quick, and before the listeners could evaluate them, we had moved on to the next. And with this rapid-fire delivery, we'd occasionally score with the biggie. That satisfied the audience. Jack Benny, in contrast, would work slowly, deliberately, but he always worked toward a sure-fire payoff. The audience was willing to listen and wait for Jack's comedy gems.

Your material must have a payoff that is reasonably priced. Certainly in any set you'll have gags or pieces of business that don't always payoff the way you would like. That's all right. Audiences will tolerate that. However, if you go too long with no payoff or a very weak one, you, the comic, will pay the price.

My advice is to listen to your act before you get onstage. Try to hear it as your audience would. Honestly evaluate each section of it. Is the punch line clever enough? Strong enough? Would it make you laugh if you were sitting out front?

One time I was working on a routine with Bob Hope. He said, "We need a punch line here." So I ad-libbed one. He looked at me. He said, "What's funny about that?" I said, "Well, it's not a fabulous joke, but it has a nice message. People will appreciate it." Hope said, "Since when did you start writing philosophy?" He wanted funny. He wanted to hear laughs.

When you analyze your act piece by piece, you'll be able to make an educated guess as to which chunks are funny enough and which aren't. Those that aren't, you either fix or you drop.

Your material should be polished.

Remember, too, that whatever material you have— whether you research it, buy it, or write it—is still only a piece of raw material. Someone supposedly asked a great sculptor how he could carve a beautiful elephant. He replied, "It's simple. You get a large block of marble and then you chip away everything that doesn't look like an elephant."

That's pretty much what you do as a stand-up comedian. You start with a big block of material that you think will work, and then you chip away everything that doesn't.

The advantage you, as a comedian, have over the elephant carver is that you can also add material. You can try different lines. You can rearrange your routine.

And that's what you should do—keep working with your material until it's sure-fire, until it's a blockbuster.

Earlier, I advised listening to your audience before you got onstage. Now I'm suggesting that you listen to your audience after you get onstage. They'll give you feedback on every piece of material that you do. Admittedly, some audiences will be different from others. Some might not laugh at a line that you know is solid. That's understandable. However, if you listen to each audience, you'll hear a pattern. You'll discover some sections that just aren't working. Those are the ones you'll want to work on.

Let me tell you one of my favorite stories about listening to your audience and reworking your comedy. Bob Hope used to do a song in his concert act about working all over the United States. He'd sing a medley of songs about the different states. He'd interrupt the music about a dozen times to do some gags about certain states.

We writers had worked and reworked this piece of material several times because Bob Hope always wanted it better, sharper, funnier.

Eventually, we had it honed almost to perfection. There was only one joke break that Hope wasn't satisfied with. He called frequently to say that the Ohio material wasn't playing. He wanted to see more jokes on his home state. We'd write them and submit them, and after his next appearance, he'd call again. "I need more stuff about Ohio."

We dreaded those calls because we were written out. We'd given him all of our best material, and it was never good enough. I asked him about that and he said, "Well, the other pieces play so well that this section is always a letdown. We have to make it as strong as the rest of the song."

So we continued to write and he continued to ask for more jokes. Finally, after one call, I conferred with the other writers, and I said, "Let's really devote ourselves to this one piece. Let's write the greatest Ohio jokes we can. That way, we'll get rid of this assignment once and for all." The writers all agreed, so we put some extra devotion into our work that day.

All of the writers were pleased with their results. When Hope called the next time, I asked if he had tried any of the new jokes for the Ohio section. He said, "Oh, yeah. There was some great material in there. I put a few of the gags in and they played terrific."

I was delighted and relieved . . . for a short time. Hope immediately added, "You know what, though? Those jokes are playing so well that now all the other pieces of the song seem a little weak."

There is no end to improving your act.

Material makes you a comedian. Good material makes you a good comedian. Outstanding material can bring you success that you haven't even dreamed of.

6

BE ORIGINAL

When I was beginning my career as a comedy writer in the Philadelphia area, I would contact any comedians who were coming to town, arrange to meet with them, and show them my material. I once made an appointment with Henny Youngman, who was in town to speak at some banquet in Center City.

While I was waiting for Mr. Youngman, I met another gentleman who was there for the same reason. He was trying to sell some jokes to Youngman, too. We introduced ourselves, discussed our writing experiences and how successful or unsuccessful we had been.

We were both delighted to be about to meet Henny Youngman. Not only was he a celebrity, but he was a potential client. He might also be our door to the big time. If he liked our stuff and told other big celebrities how good we were, well . . . the sky was the limit.

Henny was gracious and polite when he met with us. He invited us into an empty ballroom of the hotel, just off the room where he would shortly be the banquet speaker. He didn't have much time to spare so he said, "Okay, let me hear what you've got."

My new friend went first. He said proudly to Henny Youngman, "This guy has a fever of 101, you know, so he calls his doctor. The doctor tells him not to worry about it. Later he calls and says, 'Now my fever's up to 102.' The doctor says not to worry about it. He calls again and says, 'Doctor, my fever's up to 103. What should I do?'" This guy pauses for the punch line and Henny Youngman says, "When it get to 105, sell."

Now my colleague is insulted. He says, "That's my joke. Where did you hear that?"

Henny Youngman says he might have heard it in his neighborhood when he was in the fifth grade. He says, "What else do you have?"

This gentleman starts another gag and Henny Youngman supplies the punch line again. Again, my friend defends the joke, vehemently claiming it's his creation and that someone in the nefarious show-business world must have bugged his typewriter. Youngman said these gags were around long before this guy was born.

This went on for five or six jokes, until Mr. Youngman had heard enough. He said, "There's nothing here, guys. I need the funniest jokes in the world, and I need them before anybody else has heard them. I gotta go do a show." And he left.

I was left holding my portfolio of jokes. I never got a chance to audition them for Mr. Youngman or even leave copies with him. My new acquaintance shot down my presentation.

I didn't even have the heart to beg Mr. Youngman for an audience because I was embarrassed by this man's ploy, too. I had heard most of these jokes before. How could he try to get them past a performer who had been around comedy for about half a century? Why would he?

I remember when we were on the Carol Burnett writing staff, someone asked the grandmother of one of our writers what she thought her grandson did for a living. She said, in her naiveté, "Oh, he takes jokes that other people write and sells them to somebody else." We thought that was cute when we heard it, but that's exactly what this gag writer was doing—taking jokes that other people had written and trying to sell them to Henny Youngman.

There was another time that I was wounded by lack of originality. Three writers had journeyed to England with Bob Hope to write a television show he was shooting there. Most of the show had been written earlier. We were there for the last minute changes and touchups.

During the rehearsal, though, Bob Hope received word that he could get the current reigning Miss World to appear on the show. He told us three writers to do a "talk spot" for her and have it ready that afternoon. We were shooting her spot the next day. A "talk spot" is what we call those pieces where Hope would invite a guest onstage with him and they'd just chat, with Hope having a few funny lines and occasionally the guest doing a mild put-down of Hope.

The writers went to work immediately. Two of us were fairly new recruits on Bob Hope's staff; the other was a veteran of many years. The work progressed smoothly. Whenever we threw a set-up line, the veteran would come up with a fantastic joke. We'd type it in and move on to the next joke. In no time at all we had about seven pages of snappy dialogue. We made copies, sent it to Hope's room, and took our wives out for dinner.

Later that evening, I got a call from Bob Hope. He had received the material. I asked him how he liked it. He said, "It has the faint aroma of nostalgia."

Hope had done all of these jokes before, and he never forgets a punch line. He was a little miffed that we would try to sneak these past him. I couldn't say that I had never heard the jokes before and that I thought they were all terrific, but this other writer insisted that we do them. My name was one of the three at the top of the page, so I had to take at least one-third of the blame.

Anyway, the script had to be ready first thing in the morning because we were shooting the Miss World talk spot early in the day. I called the other writers and gave them the bad news. It was now quite late, so we agreed to get a good night's sleep and meet in the hotel's lobby at six in the morning to finalize a rewrite.

I couldn't sleep, knowing that I had a rewrite hanging over my head, and yet I couldn't sit up in my hotel room writing. The light would keep my wife awake all night. So I went into the bathroom with a pad and pen and stretched out in the empty bathtub, writing new jokes for Bob Hope and Miss World.

When we met in the morning, I discovered that the other young writer had done the same thing. The veteran got a good night's sleep. He wasn't as worried about his job as we were. Besides, we two "youngsters" had written plenty of jokes. We had more than enough to work into a routine. We finalized it, got it to Hope, and shot it later that day. It played very well.

The moral of these two tales is that if you're going to play in the comedy big leagues, you must be original. The emcees who played the local clubs in Philadelphia for $15 to $25 a night all did the same jokes. They were sort of public domain, there for everybody to use. But anyone who wanted to break out and become a big-time comedy star had to have fresh material and an original style. It's even more true today.

Even the non-professional raconteur at parties has the sense to say, "Stop me if you've heard this one." No one wants to hear jokes they've heard before. There's no surprise. There's no fun.

There's also no future for a stand-up comic who tells them. Oh, sometimes you can fool an audience. In fact, you can fool many audiences. However, you usually can't fool the people in the business—the ones who hire you or who critique your performances. They've seen and heard it all.

Trying to sneak something by them is not only not helpful; it's detrimental. It's like a penalty in football. If you make a long gain on an illegal play, they not only bring the ball back, but they move you backward another five, ten, or fifteen yards.

I was certainly penalized in the two instances I told you about. I lost a chance to audition my material for a well-known comic, and I had to spend the night in an uncomfortable bathtub.

I warn young comedy writers I work with to avoid material that they know is not original like they would avoid terminal writer's block. If they hand a potential client five pages of original, inventive comedy and there is one tainted gag in there, the client will become suspicious of all your material.

However, this chapter is not about plagiarism; it's about *originality*. Your jokes should certainly be different from other comedians, but so should your style and your delivery. You should be a comedy original.

Why is this originality so important? What benefits does it yield?

If you're different, you stand out.

You get noticed. I learned this when I first began to have some success as a free-lance comedy writer. I had a daytime job that restricted my travel, so most of my work was done over the telephone or through the mail. I created a logo for my stationery. Ego prompted it more than a marketing or business awareness. Also, I had an artist friend who drew it up for me for nothing. Since the price was right, I used it.

The logo was a simple drawing, no larger than a dime. It was a tiny jester's face. I put it in one corner of my stationery—the letterheads and the envelopes—along with my name and address.

To me, it was just something ornamental and a symbol of pride that I was in the business of selling jokes. I was all thrilled with my success, and this was a graphic way of reminding myself and others of my professionalism. However, years later, I discovered how important a device it was to my progress.

Two clients told me that it was that unique, distinctive drawing that set my submissions apart. In a clump of papers, the one with the drawing in the corner was easiest to locate, to find quickly. Both said they began to trust the quality of my work, and when they needed a line in a hurry, they'd search for those pages with the jester on top. This made it easier for them to use more and more of my submissions.

If you can put a distinctive stamp on your comedy material, delivery, and style, it can accomplish the same thing for you. Just as my pages stood out from a cluster of plain-white sheets, you can stand out among a gaggle of comedians.

You're more easily remembered.

If I asked you to name a comedian who works in a suit, you might mention several: Alan King, Buddy Hackett. If I wanted you to name a singer who worked in a tuxedo, you'd probably recall Frank Sinatra, Dean Martin, or Tony Bennett. But if I asked you to name a singer who worked in a white jumpsuit, you'd name Elvis Presley.

When Elvis returned to public performing in 1970 after an eight-year absence, he could easily have walked out from the wings in a nicely tailored tuxedo. Most singers at that time did. But that wasn't him. Elvis was always different, a step ahead of his time. A tux wasn't unique. He could have come onstage with his gold lamé jacket, which was his style in the '50s, but that was no longer him, either.

For his return to live performances, Elvis wanted something distinctive, unusual, original. The jumpsuit was it and it worked.

Being remembered in show business is an immense marketing tool because you're usually out of work. Even if you play two weeks in Vegas for $100,000 a week, when the fortnight is up, you're unemployed. You're usually looking for a gig. When the people who hire performers sit around and wonder who to book, you want your name to pop into their heads. That's why you want to be distinctive. Originality in your comedy will help buyers remember you.

Your originality can become your trademark.

The jumpsuit certainly became Presley's. Smashing a watermelon with a sledge hammer became Gallagher's. The wacky hair and zany costumes were Phyllis Diller's. Not getting any respect is Rodney Dangerfield's.

A trademark is welcome in show business because it says so much about you and your act so quickly. When you see a Mercedes-Benz symbol on the hood of a car, it speaks volumes. It tells you that this car is expensive, it's well-made, it's luxurious, and the owner is probably doing fairly well in whatever his or her business is.

And trademarks don't work only for the well-known performers. They work for the struggling comic, too. In fact, sometimes they work even more effectively for the aspiring performers because they need a symbol since their names are not yet established. For instance, you're thinking of going to a local comedy club. You ask someone, "Who's appearing there?" They tell you Joe Doaks and Loretta Smith. You say, I never heard of them. Your friend tells you, "They're good. You've seen them before. Joe Doaks is the guy who does the 'Milk' routine and Loretta Smith does that great 'Getting engaged' monologue."

You don't know their names, but you know their trademark routines.

If you're unique, you don't suffer in comparison to the original.

You are the original. Suppose, for example, that you are a pretty talented singer, and you decide that you want to work wearing a spangled jumpsuit with a large, upturned collar. That's your privilege. It's not copyrighted and no one owns the right to appear onstage in a white jumpsuit.

However, what are people going to say after your performance? "He's pretty good, but he's no Elvis Presley." You're begging them to compare you to Elvis. Not only are they going to compare your voice to Elvis's voice, but they're going to measure your performance against the Presley legend. I don't care how talented you are, there's no way you're going to outstrip the King of Rock 'n' Roll with one performance.

You, like everyone else, have seen dozens of Elvis impersonators. Some of them are pretty bad; many of them are laughable. A few of them, though, are believable. Would you ever hire one? Sure, if you wanted a novelty act. It's like hiring a clown to stand outside a fast-food store and wave at the cars that drive by. Have you ever seen one that was better than the original? Better than Elvis? Have you ever seen one that you would want to offer a recording contract to? Have you ever seen one that you would want to play the leading role in a movie you were about to produce? No, you see them and you forget them. Elvis made an impression on you; the impersonators don't.

Admittedly, this is the extreme, but young performers do this to a lesser degree quite frequently. They slavishly mimic the performers they admire.

Now there's nothing wrong with being inspired by good performers, learning from them, and even trying to emulate their talent. But the trick is to incorporate some of their attributes into your own style of performing. Adding your own flair to an accepted style is a form of originality. We'll talk about it a little later in this chapter. But copying a legendary performer so much that your act amounts to a cheap imitation is counterproductive.

You'd prefer to have an audience say, "You know, he reminds me a little bit of Elvis," rather than, "He's no Elvis."

Being an original performer forces you to work harder on your act, on your material.

Earlier we said that the Magic Bullet to success in show business is to be good. Being unique forces you to work harder at being good.

Why? Because you have nothing to fall back on. Your own quality is the measure of your success; therefore, it had better be good.

Consider again the Elvis impersonator. He needs a cheap jumpsuit, sideburns, and maybe a pair of sunglasses. That's it. Once the white jumpsuit is paid for, that's as good as this act is going to get.

But if you're an honest-to-goodness one-of-a-kind stand-up comedian, you owe it to yourself to keep your material incisive, to keep your style fresh, to keep your act sharp. You're it, baby, so you'd better be good. There's nothing wrong with putting that kind of pressure on yourself—if you're determined to make it, that is.

I should point out, too, that being original doesn't necessarily mean reinventing the wheel. You don't have to be so radically different from anything that went before that you're totally bizarre. There are different forms and levels of originality.

Of course, if you do come up with something that has never been seen or heard before, that's original. However, you can also improve something to make it fresh and different. You can add to something that already exists. You can combine elements of things that already exist to create something unique.

For instance, the microwave oven was a new and innovative way of cooking, different from anything that went before. Yet the pop-up toaster was an innovation, too. Toasters existed, but not one that would pop the bread up when it was toasted. Then even those were improved upon. They added controls so your toast could be light or dark, browned just the way you like it. And, finally, they combined pop-up toasters with toaster ovens.

I've been harsh on Elvis impersonators, but there's even some benefit in using the Presley style to build upon. When Elvis began in the '50s, he was a mover. When he sang, he gyrated. That was how he got the nickname "Elvis the Pelvis," and it was why Ed Sullivan only showed him from the waist up when he guested on that show.

Now, Billy Ray Cyrus is a mover. When he sings, he gyrates. He's using a little bit of Elvis, but he's combining it with Billy Ray. It results in a style that's different and certainly successful.

Now let's talk a little bit about how you go about becoming a unique, individualized, original performer.

We'll talk about three areas:

1. Your appearance
2. Your delivery
3. Your subject matter

Your appearance

Like it or not, the way you look is part of your act. It can influence your performance. I once attended a convention where a motivational speaker addressed the attendees. He told each of us in the audience that with dedication and positive thinking, we could do anything and be anything we wanted. The person next to me leaned over and said, "I guess this guy *wants* to be twenty-five pounds overweight."

Here was a gentleman who was preaching self-improvement, ways to make one's life ideal. Yet he was standing up there with a belt that drooped and a belly that protruded. His appearance was much more eloquent than his speech was.

For your professional attire to be effective, it should be consistent with your personality, your style, and your message. Andrew Dice Clay looks perfectly normal in chains and black leather. Bob Newhart in the same outfit would look ridiculous.

Your professional attire can also be distinctive. Mort Sahl worked in a V-neck sweater at a time when most comedians wore a shirt and tie. Sam Kinnison wore a beret and a long overcoat. Phyllis Diller wanted to make an impression the minute she walked out from the wings, so she wore bizarre, funny looking costumes and had jokes about them.

Arsenio Hall is unique, even when he appears on his show in a coat and tie. He wears nicely tailored suits, but in bright, vibrant colors. They're tasteful, but quite different. Jackie Gleason, when he hosted his television shows, wore well-tailored suits. However, he always had a fresh-cut flower in his lapel. It was an elegant, distinctive touch.

So many of the comedy-club comics look the same— as if they borrow clothes from one another for their comedy sets. You can dress any way that's comfortable onstage, anyway that you feel is you. However, it's nice to have a distinctive touch, something that sets you apart from all the other comics. It may be a distinctive wardrobe like Arsenio Hall's or it may be a subtle touch like Jackie Gleason's flower. The particulars will have to come from you, but it is worth some thought.

Here is a slight warning, though: Be careful in your selection because you may have to live with it. For example, you may decide to wear a finely tailored suit, except with oversized gorilla feet instead of shoes. Fine. That's different, and it will certainly get noticed and talked about. But, will you be able to meet the Queen of England in such a get-up? Will you be able to act as Master of

Ceremonies for the Oscar telecast in such garb? Will you be selected as a romantic lead in a major motion picture wearing such footwear? Think about it before committing.

Your delivery

We spoke earlier in the chapter about the sameness of the delivery of comedy-club comics. They want to read each punch line with the same intonation and with the same gestures and takes. Every reading comes with its own rimshot. To sound original, you must find a way to deliver your lines without that comedy-club dialect.

When I was a high-school kid, I had to study Shakespeare. All of us hated it. The lines made no sense, and when we read them in class, we all read them in the same poetic rhythm. They're magnificent lines, but they do have a cadence to them that can be sickening.

Then the teacher took us all to see Laurence Olivier in *Hamlet.* What an eye-opener. These lines actually made sense. They had passion. They were interesting, exciting, dramatic. All of us high-school kids actually enjoyed Shakespeare.

In the classroom, we read them with a sing-songy tempo. Olivier and his fellow actors delivered them with meaning. They reacted to their fellow performers and they felt the lines as they delivered them.

That's the difference between a comedian who delivers one-liners in the predictable, sing-songy cadence of the comedy club and a performer who actually *talks* to the audience, who puts some emotion into the humor.

Jay Leno once advised beginning comics to learn how to talk first, before doing any funny material. Get familiar with standing before a crowd and speaking. Be willing to speak extemporaneously whenever you get the chance, or to stand up and read if the opportunity presents itself. It's good advice and good practice.

You might also read a little Shakespeare aloud. You

won't find a more economical writer, and it's good practice to find the meaning in his words and read them with some feeling.

Also, try reciting some poetry aloud. Here you have to resist the urge to read the lines to tempo, to almost sing the cadence. Try instead to read the meaning of the lines, as if it were prose instead of poetry.

Finally, struggle to resist the comedy-club inflection in all of your punch lines. Experiment with different ways of delivering the line.

Eventually, you'll find your own comfortable delivery and that will become your distinct, unique style.

Your subject matter

Once again, there's a sameness to this. Years ago, the nightclub comics used to talk about "my wife," "my lazy brother-in-law," and betting on the horses. Today they have different topics, but everyone is doing them. For a while, everyone was kidding about the commercials on TV. The female comics all talk about PMS and women's problems. If you listen to several comics on the same bill at a local comedy club, you'll hear the same topics in many of the comedians' routines.

That's the brilliance of someone like Jerry Seinfeld—he takes common occurrences and finds the humor in them. His subject matter is different from that of everyone else. Why? You and I do the same things that Seinfeld does.

George Carlin can do hilarious routines that are unique. He does them about the language that airlines use, strange phrases that people use. He even has one bit about "stuff."

How come they see the fun in these things and we don't? We still talk about the same things that every other comedian is talking about. "Have you ever noticed that all the clerks who work at the all-night convenience stores are foreigners?"

One way to find new and different things to talk about is to be alert and observant. Focus in particular areas to uncover things to write about. I recently did an article for comedy writers that listed ten sure-fire ways to stimulate ideas. The basic premise was that the more you can focus on a smaller area, the easier it is to extract ideas from it. Following is a shortened version of those ten ideas to help stimulate comedy-writing creativity.

1. Focus on the hours of your day. Break your day into segments of two hours each. From 12 midnight till 2 A.M., from 2 to 4 in the morning, and so on. Focus on one of those segments, anyone you like, and analyze what you do during that time. Find some things that you can write comedy about. From midnight till 2 A.M. you might raid the refrigerator, you might dream, you might have to get up to go to the bathroom, your dog may wake you to go outside to go to the bathroom, you might think you hear burglars. You might find any number of areas that you could focus on to extract humor from.

2. Focus on different places you go. Track a typical day and list the number of places you visit. Make a list of these for future reference. There might be the post office, the department store, the doctor, the dentist, the police station, whatever. Now when it's time to create, pick one of these and analyze it. Find the fun in it. Do a routine about one of them.

You can also divide your own home into segments and analyze each one. You'll find some humor in your kitchen, bathroom, closet, anyplace—if you work at it a little bit.

3. Break the world into different geographic sections. Find out as much as you can about certain parts of the world that you know little about. I'll bet you'll find something worth a few laughs in whichever place you select.

4. Your past is worth rethinking, too. Break your life down into five-year segments. Think about each one—what you did during that time in your life, what you learned, what you would do differently. Keep these as a reference, then when you have to create some funny material, select one and focus on it. I guarantee you'll find some fun in it.

5. How about all the people you've known in your lifetime. They're all different and probably worth talking about. Think about as many as you can and list their good and bad points, the traits you admire and the ones you detest. When you're stuck for new comedy ideas, a look back on this reference file should inspire you.

6. There's a world of interesting facts that you can talk about. Bill Cosby did a funny routine about how Custer and the Indians tossed a coin to set the rules for the battle at Little Big Horn. Custer lost the toss. Bob Newhart did a funny routine about Sir Walter Raleigh trying to sell his bosses on the idea of tobacco. They thought he was nuts. There's fun in many segments of history. When you want some ideas, just stick a pin into a page of the encyclopedia, open it up, and find some humor about whatever is on that page. It might take a little creativity, but when you're done it will be different.

7. Dissect the human body. I don't mean literally, but figuratively. Focus on the head, the trunk, the extremities. Is there something in each of those parts that might generate some humor? I'm sure there is if you look hard enough. Separate it into the different senses—smell, sight, touch, taste, hearing. There's something funny about each of those. Now think about various functions. The digestive system, the cardio-vas-

cular system, and so on. You'll get some jokes on all of those.

8. Fantasies you've had over the years should lead to humor. What do you daydream about now? What did you daydream about when you were younger? Have any of your daydreams come true for you? There's raw material for humor in all of those.

9. Dissect the year into twelve parts. Call them months, if you like. Now think about them. What happens in January? February? The rest of the months? You should be able to stimulate some ideas for each of the twelve calendar months.

10. Finally, much humor is revenge. It's a way of getting even with the world for injustices, so think of some of the things in this world that annoy you. List them and then when it's time to write your comedy, take out the list and be funny.

Naturally, these are only suggestions, and they're certainly not all-inclusive. That's the nice thing about originality—it can't be confined. Once you limit it to a certain area, you open up all the non-included areas for creativity. If you draw a circle on a piece of paper, the inside of that circle is limited. What's outside the circle is infinite.

What has already been done in comedy is within the circle. You have a limitless range of possibilities outside that circle. They're all fresh, new, and different. All you have to do is work to find them and make them a part of your comedy.

7
BUILD YOUR REPERTOIRE

Somewhere during my studies or in some of my reading, I discovered that the human body completely renovates itself over a period of about seven years. Hair and fingernails grow out and are cut away. Cells die and are replaced by new cells. The process is gradual but ongoing and after approximately seven years is complete. That means that after that time, you have an entirely new body. You're a different person. So if there are any readers out there that I borrowed money from seven and a half years ago, tough.

But it's a pretty efficient way of keeping your body fresh and new. It's painless and effortless. It would be nice if cars maintained themselves that way, wouldn't it? It would circumvent that painful process of trying to sell or trade in your old car and haggling with the dealer to purchase a new one at a fair, or less than fair, price.

It's certainly better than having the replacement of your old body regulated by the government. You'd have to go to some bureaucratic office and stand in line for hours on end to trade in your old carcass and get a new one.

No, the incremental, undetectable replacement process is the best. It's also a good way to build your comedy repertoire and to fine-tune it.

If you're a raw beginner with the desire to be a comic but no material, you begin to stockpile comedy material slowly, piece by piece. An old proverb advises that the journey of a thousand miles begins with the first step. You begin gathering two hours of dependable comedy by developing that first three-minute chunk. When you're satisfied with it, you create another three minutes of laughs, then another three minutes. Eventually, you'll have a set that you can trust, and enough for a second set.

Constructing a solid chunk of comedy is an ongoing process, one of trial and error, write and rewrite, test and polish.

I've written for nightclubs, variety shows, sitcoms, and a few movies, and I know that the first draft is always the easiest. The grueling, time-consuming work is usually in the rewrite—more correctly I should say, the rewrites.

Looking at what you've written, analyzing it, testing it, and reshaping it is what makes a chunk of comedy effective.

How do you go about assembling that first three-minute chunk? Let's assume that you've decided on a comedy style and persona, or at least that you've decided on giving a certain style and persona a try. Let's assume, too, that you've decided on a topic to talk about. Now you want to start developing the lines.

You begin by overwriting. That means, if you need three minutes of material, you write six minutes, or nine minutes, or whatever. If Bob Hope needs five or six lines of specific material at the beginning of a personal appearance, he'll call his writers. He may have three writers or he may have ten. He'll call them all and say, "I need a few things about so and so or such and such." Each writer takes notes and then writes twenty to thirty lines on that specific topic. Hope winds up with 50 to 300 lines on just that topic. From that he selects five or six. With that many lines to choose from, you'd guess that the half-dozen he uses would be pretty good.

You do the same thing on a smaller scale. You overproduce. You gather much more material on your topic than you want or need, then you select the choicest material. If you've done a good job of assembling the material, you should be able to cull some funny lines for your short chunk.

Why overwrite? If Bob Hope needs only a handful of gags, why doesn't he just call one dependable writer and have him or her submit a handful of gags? Because another writer may just think of a better joke. A few other writers may attack the topic from a different point of view and give it a unique slant. By getting as many gags as he reasonably can to select from, Hope is assured of getting the top-quality material for the few remarks that he must make.

Overwriting helps you in similar ways.

It forces you to focus on your topic.

If you need a joke about getting a traffic ticket, it's relatively easy to find one through research or even to write one in a hurry. But is that the best anecdote or one-liner on the subject? Probably not. There might be better ones available. By forcing yourself to think about your topic until you either write or find lots of material on that subject, you're conning yourself into being more creative, into researching longer and harder. You're forcing yourself to gather better material.

It prevents you from quitting too soon.

This is the biggest error young comedians and young comedy writers make. They give up on a project before they do their best work. They settle for "good enough" and never allow themselves to find "the best."

Sometimes I submit my material to Bob Hope by reading the lines to him. Many times he'll listen to a line, wave his hand back and forth, and say, "That's just fair. That *might* work." Then he'll say, "What else have you got?" or

"Let's try a few more." He rarely settles for good enough.

Once you decide that your work is done on a given project, you give up all chance of improving it. You're accepting what you have as the absolute best that you can deliver. However, if you continue to work on the project, you just might come up with better and funnier lines. If you do, you substitute them; if you don't, you haven't lost any quality. You can still use the original lines.

Gathering much more than you need gives you a better selection.

You wouldn't shop in a clothing store that offers only one suit or one dress. You want to consider a few and decide which looks best on you. You should do the same in considering comedy material.

Overwriting provides backup material.

Invariably, you'll find that some of the material you've included is not working the way you want it to. Your routine will need some editing. Then, you may want to reconsider a few of the lines that you didn't select the first time. Your backup material may come in handy as you polish your routine.

So, your first step is to gather much more material than you'll need, either by writing it, buying it, or researching it.

Next, you want to assemble that into a logical, continuous routine. I suggest you begin by selecting only those lines that you feel are worthy. Be ruthless and eliminate the weaker material. Save it, but don't include it in this first draft.

Now arrange the material you do like into a routine. Give it a logical flow. In other words, arrange it into a conversation with your audience that feels natural to you.

At this point, you might discover that you need additional material. You might have to find ways to blend from one line to another, from one point to another. Take the time to create those transitions.

You might find, too, that you need additional material. There might be gaps in the logical flow of your story. If there are, you must take time to fill them in.

When you're finished with this block of work, you should have a chunk of material, lasting anywhere from three to six minutes, that you're satisfied with. It should be a piece of material that you feel comfortable presenting to an audience.

However, that's when the real fine-tuning begins—when you present it to an audience. You'll let them guide you in your rewrite. Perhaps you'll find that the piece starts out like gangbusters and then slows down when you reach a certain point. Okay, that area needs work. Maybe it should be dropped, replaced, or repositioned. Try all of those. Maybe that area of the chunk needs a rewrite. Some of those lines that you discarded might work better than the ones you selected. Try them.

At this stage, you play with the piece. You add, subtract, rearrange. Many times, you'll discover that pieces that you ad-lib while you're in the spotlight work better than the segments that you slaved over. Fine, incorporate them. Find out what makes the chunk better and what makes it worse. It's like going to the eye doctor for an examination. "Better like this? or better like this?" Let your audience give you the answers.

When this becomes a solid chunk of material that you can depend on, start working on your next piece. Actually, you should be gathering material for your next piece while you're polishing this. Developing your material should be an ongoing process.

Some beginners may wonder how they can practice a routine before an audience when they don't have an audience. It doesn't have to be a paying crowd or even in a club. You can try material out on your friends. Anytime you have people listening, try this chunk of material, or a part of it, on them. You'll get some feedback that could prove useful.

Now let's assume you've been doing comedy awhile. You have a set that you use and it works fairly well. That's fine, but it can probably be better, and if not, then you're going to need more material sooner or later anyway because with that good an act, you're going to get famous and get heavy exposure. You'll need a brand-new act when that happens.

If you want to build new material, you go through the process we just discussed above. With a solid act already working for you, you can work in short three-to-six-minute chunks without harming the effectiveness of your performance. You can gradually work on separate pieces until they're the same quality as the rest of your act.

Begin with the weakest point.

Regardless of how powerful your act is, some part of it is weaker than some other part. You start with that slower spot and concentrate on it. Make changes and try them out. Add material, subtract material. Try different things until you find the magic formula that works.

When you build up that section of the act, what happens? Another section now becomes the weaker part of your act. Work on that. Make it better.

What's the natural result of all this? Each part of the act keeps getting better and better; consequently, your whole performance improves.

Once I was a reluctant participant in this process, but this story does illustrate that it works.

I was traveling with the Hope troupe on a peacetime

jaunt to military bases around the world. We visited Berlin at the time when the wall was being dismantled, and we were even welcomed into Moscow to do a show. Hope did a song medley with Rosemary Clooney that was a creative, but very mechanical, piece of comedy. I say mechanical not disparagingly but in the sense that the piece depended on the music—the melody and the lyrics. Therefore, it couldn't be tampered with too much.

To give you an example, Rosemary Clooney would sing to Hope, "Why do I love you?" and Hope would sing back boastfully, "Because I'm lovely to look at, delightful to hold, and heaven to kiss." This would get a nice laugh from the audience.

There were about twenty-two dialogue exchanges within the piece, all of which consisted of lyrics from easily recognized songs. It worked nicely.

Not nicely enough for Bob Hope, though. After one session he said to me, "Iit would be nice if we got bigger laughs in that piece." So, I came up with one change. Hope sang, "Because I'm lovely to look at, delightful to hold, and I've had all my shots." The military audience loved this and laughed louder.

Now Bob Hope wanted more changes in the piece. I argued that the beauty of the piece was that we were using real lyrics from real songs. Tampering with them too much would not only ruin the creativity of the piece, but might hurt the laughs because the songs might become unrecognizable.

Hope said, "What are you talking about? You just got major laughs with that one rewrite." I said, "That was changing the third line. That song was already established. Other ones in the routine aren't. If you change them, you destroy the flow."

Hope said, "Just get more laughs."

So I worked on that piece. I suggested changes. Hope would sometimes ad-lib a line that worked. Rosemary Clooney would throw in a different line occasionally.

Those that worked we kept.

By the time the trip was over, this musical segment changed drastically. It went from a cute musical medley to a solid piece of comedy with some big laughs throughout.

Why? Because Hope wanted bigger laughs and we all concentrated on it, worked on it, and gradually improved it.

That's the same process you have to employ on your act—whether you're just beginning or whether you've been behind the mike for several years.

Allow your material to expand.

Analyze the material you already have. Look at the routines that you're presently using, ones that are working well for you, and go inside them for inspiration.

A magazine writer once told me that he believed every article he sold contained ideas for at least three other articles. For example, if he sold an article about a certain shopping district in a certain city, that article would list several of the stores in that shopping district. Now he might isolate one of those stores. When did it first appear in this area? Who founded it? Who does the buying for it? If it features a certain kind of clothing, he might research that and write an article about it. He might find out the history of the building that store is in and discover that would make an interesting article. In other words, he uses this one piece he has written to generate ideas for other pieces.

You can do the same with your comedy material. Suppose, for example, you do a chunk of material about buying a puppy. It can be working beautifully so that it needs no repairs or alterations. Fine. The audience loves it. Then build on that.

This audience may want to know how this puppy behaved after it grew up. If you bought this creature to become a watchdog, you might do a routine on how it succeeded or failed as a watchdog. You may have acquired this puppy because you didn't have much success with the pet you had before—a hamster, goldfish, whatever.

How did this puppy affect your life after you got it home? Does it insist on sleeping in your bed? Are you allergic to it? Do your other pets get along with it?

You get the idea. If you've got any piece of material that is reaching the audience, it should inspire similar or related routines. Working on these can build your comedy repertoire.

You can see how this has worked for other successful comics. Tim Allen probably had a routine about power tools and the macho man that got lots of laughs, so he kept building on that premise. Soon he became the power-tool comic. That begot "Home Improvement."

Roseanne Arnold probably built on her material about being the long-suffering housewife and mother.

You can probably study the routine you're doing presently and discover which portions of it are the most successful. From those, you can begin to list a whole network of related ideas that you might begin to develop into comedy routines.

You notice that this is building on your comedy strengths. Earlier I suggested strengthening the weaker parts of your act; now I'm telling you that you can also build on the strong parts of your comedy. By using both of these tools, you're pulling your entire act up. You're making it stronger and stronger, better and better, funnier and funnier.

Of course, once you develop new routines based on successful routines you're already doing, you go through the same process of preparing, polishing, and refining. You overwrite and select the best material. You organize that into a presentable piece. Then you analyze the piece each time you present it and fine-tune the comedy based on audience reaction.

The secret to developing more and better comedy

material is constant vigilance. It's a continuing effort.
You're never finished.

8

SIT IN YOUR OWN AUDIENCE

I've played tennis for a number of years. I've always considered myself a fairly competent player who moves with quickness and grace, who maintains good balance, and has a swing that's not overpowering, but more delicate, perhaps with the finesse of a John McEnroe.

That's what I always considered—until I enrolled in a tennis teaching program that used a video camera. All of us students went onto the court and hit a few forehands and backhands while the staff videotaped us. Then we sat in a classroom while our performance was evaluated by an instructor.

I was short, fat, and bald, and I didn't look like a professional on the tennis court. I looked more like a tourist in Tijuana. I ran like a pregnant duck, and I swung the racquet like I was swatting flies.

It was the first time I had ever seen myself playing tennis, and it was nothing at all like the picture I had in my mind as I played.

Seeing myself from the sidelines projected an entirely different image. It startled me and distressed me. It added considerably to my bar bill that evening. I came, I saw, and now I wanted to forget.

I realized now why my tennis game wasn't terrorizing opponents. To my mind's eye, I was hitting shots with accuracy and ferocity. I was in the correct position at all times, presenting a formidable obstacle to the person on the other side of the net. However, I was the only one seeing this image. Everyone who was playing me was seeing the real image—a cute, harmless, little person with a racquet.

Those who perform stand-up rarely see the real image, either. They see their entire performance from the stage and visualize how they look. That visualization is usually distorted. It's retouched with wishful thinking. It's tainted with how we wish we looked and sounded.

As a comedy writer, I'm always amused by those comics who come offstage with a complaint: "Boy, this is the worst audience in the world. There's nothing but a bunch of stiffs out there. The monkeys in the zoo couldn't get laughs from this crowd if you dropped a bottle of Scotch in their drinking water."

Maybe the audience this night wasn't laughing, but the question is, Did you give them anything to laugh at? Did you say anything funny? Did your jokes have punch lines? If you were sitting in the audience this evening, would you have laughed at your performance?

This is a tremendously important question for a stand-up comic to ask because if *you* honestly wouldn't laugh at this performance, how can you expect these people to laugh at it?

I've heard comics bewildered that no one laughed at a certain routine. Then I reviewed the routine and solved the puzzle: There was nothing in there to laugh at. The jokes just weren't funny enough. They weren't the kind that would make a crowd erupt with laughter.

You have to sit in your own audience. You have to view your performance as the viewing customers would view it. Not as you think they would see it, or as you hope they would see it, but as they actually see and hear it.

Obviously, you can't be two places at one time. If you're on the stage, you can't be sitting in the third row, too. But you can read over your material and try to hear it as the paying customers will hear it.

I've worked with Bob Hope many times when the writers or the producers would suggest an idea for the show. Hope would say, "No. I don't want that. That's just a waste of time. It slows things down." He was seeing this show as the viewers at home would watch it on their TV set. What we were suggesting might have been nice, artsy, dramatic. What Hope wanted, though, was a grabber, something that hit those people in their living room. He was seeing his television special from the viewer's living room.

That's how you have to see, or more importantly, hear your comedy set.

What exactly do I mean by "sitting in your own audience?" I mean you have to review your routine line by line, punch line by punch line, analyzing each potential joke. Ask yourself, "Will this get a laugh from an ordinary audience?" Some jokes may be clever, they may be cute, they may be ironic, but will they produce a laugh? Will they force an audience to respond? And you do this *before* you present the routine to the public.

Admittedly, you're only guessing, but it's an educated guess. You know comedy, you've studied it and been around it. You surely know a good joke when you hear one or read one in a book. You should know one when you read it in your own routine—provided you're being honest with yourself.

Sometimes you'll guess wrong. That's all right. That can be fixed as you polish the routine. You may think a line is a sure-fire laugh-getter and it fizzles. Okay, you replace it or you rewrite it. That's part of polishing a routine, refining it as you perform before an audience.

What you desperately want to avoid, though, is getting before your listeners with material that you have to admit is substandard.

Read over your material and make sure you've got some big jokes in your routine and that they're spaced well. You don't want to go too long between "biggies." You might lose your audience.

There are various ways you can do this. You can rate the punch lines in your routine on a scale of one to five or one to ten. You can put a plus beside the jokes that are pretty dependable and a double-plus beside the ones that you are positive will get big laughs.

Devise your own system. The important thing is not the procedure but that you have reviewed your material and can assure yourself, with a reasonable amount of certainty, that you have confidence in this routine.

You've heard stories, I'm sure, of show-business performers who were alleged prima donnas. They caused trouble on the set with impossible demands, walked off sets, and the like. Some of those stories are true. However, I've also worked with stars who were labelled troublemakers because they refused to do material that was not well-written.

Someone tried to give them material that wasn't up to their professional standards. The writers or producers got lazy and decided to give them a script that was just "good enough." They balked and demanded a rewrite. Is that being temperamental, or is it simply insisting on quality?

Once I worked with Roseanne Arnold. She was very gracious and cooperative during rehearsal. She did question one line she had in the script. She didn't understand it. There was no way she could have understood it because it was a mistake. Her line referred back to an earlier line that had been deleted; consequently, what she said made no sense.

I rewrote it and gave her the revised script right before she was to go onstage. She accepted the change and said to me, "You know another line that I think is really lousy?"

I had to laugh that she could be that outspoken. After all, she was talking to the head writer, the person responsible for the script. I asked which line and she told me. Again, she was right. It was a lousy line. She suggested an alternate that was very funny, so we put it in the script.

Roseanne wasn't being cantankerous when she called the joke "lousy." She was being playful with me, but she was also keeping a close eye on her part of the script. She didn't like this line and she didn't want to say it. To me, that's professionalism.

You must be honest enough to look at your own script and say, "This joke is lousy."

I knew one producer who read situation-comedy scripts and underlined each guaranteed laugh with a red pencil. When he was finished, he would leaf through the pages again. Any page that didn't have at least three red lines on it had to be rewritten. He created a magical mathematical formula that he felt helped the pace of his comedy shows—at least three solid laughs per page.

I've worked with some comics who wanted me to listen to a script of theirs and rate each of the potential punch lines. I'd mark each of them on a scale from one to five. Other writers who worked for him would do the same. We'd get a consensus of the strength of the jokes that way.

Together we would analyze the results to make sure that there were a good number of fours and fives in the script and that they were fairly evenly spaced. He even wanted to be sure that the jokes built properly, that a two led up to a three, then to the bigger jokes.

If we had too many low-rated gags in one spot, we'd drop some or replace them or rewrite them to make them stronger.

This comic didn't want to give the audience any excuse not to like the performance.

I worked with another performer who would sit down with the writers to analyze a script immediately after a rehearsal. We'd read through the script line by line and note where we might get a better line. We'd note lines that didn't work. Those we'd replace. We'd identify spaces in the script where there was no punch line, but there should be.

When we were done combing through the script, the writers would have several places marked for new or better lines. We'd all work on jokes for those areas, and then we'd pick the best of the new submissions to be included in the final draft of the sketch.

Most of the writing teams that I've worked with in television make that their final run-through of a script. The beginning, middle, and end has already been worked out. The plot points have all been developed. Now the project is to make the script funnier. Crank more or bigger laughs into it.

As a group, we go through the script page by page and line by line. We question jokes. "Is this funny enough or do you think we can come up with a better line here?" "Let's get a piece of business for this section." "I think this line screams for a payoff. We don't have one. Let's get one."

After we've all voiced our opinions and discussed the pros and cons, we have a script that's been marked with several areas for rewriting. Then again as a group, we'll begin throwing new lines, new set-ups, whatever we agreed that we needed. We begin with the first marked page and continue to the last one. When we've rewritten all of the marked pages, we turn the script in for retyping and issue the new pages to the performers.

That's what you should do alone or with any writing or creative team that you have. That's sitting in your own audience.

What are the advantages to viewing and listening to your act from your audience's point of view?

You'll know what you're doing.

You're familiar with your material before you put it before the public. That's good. It's professional and it shows you've got savvy. It's also the safest way to walk onstage. Airline pilots always inspect the aircraft before sitting in the cockpit. I don't know what they're looking for, but they do. They want to glance at certain important mechanisms and assure themselves that they're in working order.

Even in the cockpit, they go through an itemized checklist. Again, I don't know what they check, but they do. They're not only in charge of that aircraft, but they're also going to be sitting in it—right up front. They want to be sure that all systems are go before they try to get it off the ground.

You want to be certain, too, that your routine, your act, your material is in good working order before you get behind the microphone. It's just a good, safe, operating procedure.

I remember one time as a young writer when I didn't review my work before handing it in. I wrote a sketch—a very funny sketch, I thought—and handed it in to the producers. They read it and told me it needed a lot more work.

I argued. "That's a very funny sketch," I told them. "There're a lot of laughs in there. You tell me just exactly where that sketch needs work."

Neither one of them answered me; they just began leafing through the pages I'd handed in. Page by page they glanced at it. Finally, they stopped. One looked up and said, "I just counted twelve pages where the star of the show doesn't say anything."

That's a glaring, amateurish, unforgivable error to leave any performer onstage with nothing to say or do for that many pages. I would have caught the error if I had not only read the sketch but "viewed" it as a member of the audience. If I had truly "seen" the sketch being performed before handing it in, I would have noticed the awkward position I left the headliner in.

You'll improve the quality of your act.

You're going through it to get better jokes, and more jokes. Presumably, you'll get more and bigger laughs. For a comedian, that's good.

Of course, you'll still have some work to do on your routine. We said earlier that you'll refine your material as you go, as you perform. If that's true, you might wonder, Why work on this first draft so much? Why nit-pick before you even get in front of an audience since you're going to rewrite it afterward?

Because you want dependable feedback from this audience. You get that by presenting the best possible performance to begin with.

Producers sometimes have the same problem with writers. Almost every script that free-lance writers hand in to producers is handed back to them along with notes and suggestions for a rewrite.

Writers know this, and a few of them might hand in a slipshod first draft knowing that they can do their brilliant work on the one that counts, their second and final draft.

When writers do this, it's not fair. Producers depend on a quality first draft. With that, their notes are more meaningful, and the next draft and subsequent rewrites are of better quality. It's also unwise for writers to cheat on the first draft. Several producers, when auditioning new writers, ask to see a first draft, not a second or final draft. They want to see the writer's own work, not the script that was prompted by producers' notes or staff rewrites.

Likewise, you're being fair to your act by reviewing your material before you get it onstage.

You'll improve the pacing of your act.

You'll get the laughs started and you'll keep them going. You'll keep the audience interested. Remember, you can lose your listeners in comedy, and once you do, you have to work hard to get them back.

By reviewing your material, by sitting in your own audience, you've got a better shot at keeping the laughs flowing.

You'll keep weak material out of your routine.

That's important because it's often the weak material that turns an audience against you.

I recommend to beginning writers that they avoid fatal mistakes in their spec scripts. Even though producers are eager to find good scripts, they're busy. Consequently, when they read a bad script, they quickly discard it and get on to reading the next. If a writer has a glaring flaw in the script, an amateurish mistake, that's the only excuse the producer needs to abandon that spec script. Regardless of how much good writing is in there, one mistake can cost the writer the assignment.

The same can be true for stand-up comedians. You might have some truly inventive, funny material in your set, but if the audience hears a few clunkers, that's all they need to dismiss you.

If you go over your material and sort out the slow spots and the weaker material, you're not allowing them to give up on you. You're forcing them to listen. That's good.

You're getting the jump on your competition.

The race for success in stand-up comedy is cut-throat. Everyone wants to get to the top as fast as he or she can. Everyone wants to be the one singled out by the audience and by the buyers. Everyone wants to be noticed by the networks.

People notice quality—especially in today's comedy. There are many young comic hopefuls out there. Quality—good, funny, inventive material—will make you a standout among them. In other words, if you're good, you will be noticed.

Usually after watching comedians perform in a comedy club, my companions and I will ask, "Who did you like best?" We compare and rate the several performers we've seen. We're looking for the quality.

If you polish your routine before you step onstage, you're increasing your chances of being the one that sparkles, the one who's singled out as the best. Audiences will appreciate the effort you put into your material simply because its quality will demand their attention.

And when audiences notice you, the people in the business will notice you. That's when you're talked about, when you get better bookings, when you get better offers.

It helps you to develop a professional attitude about your performances.

You'll want to be a standout each time you step onstage. You'll begin to demand it of yourself. You'll learn to think about your material, your performance. You'll care about your audience.

You'll become a better comic.

There's one other item I want to mention about sitting in your own audience. When I do mention it you'll think, "That's so obvious, why even bring it up?" I know because that's what I thought when the producer of "Laugh-In" first mentioned it to our writing staff. Later I realized the wisdom of his admonition.

Be sure, as you're reviewing your material from the audience's vantage point, that with each joke you're telling the listeners when to laugh. See, I told you you would say, "That's so obvious, why even bring it up?"

You're right. It is obvious. It's so obvious, though, that many performers—not only beginners, but veterans, too—forget it.

What I mean by it is that each punch line, each piece of business, must have a place where the audience knows when to laugh. One fairly well-known comic performed at a comedy club. He began his set by telling the audience that a really good comedian could get laughs reading names out of a phone book. With that, he sat down in a chair, opened a phone book, and began reciting names. He employed no pieces of business. He didn't change his inflection, gestures, or facial expressions. He sat there and read names out of a phone book.

Some people laughed. Some got hysterical with laughter. Others stared around the room in confusion.

It's a crazy, zany, audacious thing to do. It's funny to hear that some comic had the audacity to try such a gimmick.

But imagine yourself in that audience. When do you begin to laugh? After the third name? The tenth? The one hundredth? You're not sure, are you?

When do you stop laughing? Again, you're not sure.

There's no place in this routine where the comic tells the audience to laugh. There's no spot in this act where laughter erupts. It sort of happens—a titter here, a chuckle there. That's the comedy of this routine—that there is no comedy.

Good, solid, belly-rolling laughter happens when you tell people when to laugh. Consider these jokes:

> I used to work in a fire-hydrant factory.
> You couldn't park anywhere near the
> place.   — Steven Wright

> My boyfriend and I broke up. He wanted
> to get married and I didn't want him to.
>   — Rita Rudner

> Weather forecast for tonight—dark.
>   — George Carlin

These are funny, well-constructed lines. Notice that each one has a place where the audience knows when to laugh. There is a definite *punch* line in each. In Steven Wright's line, the surprise comes with the second part of the joke. The surprise in Rita Rudner's gag is contained in the last part of the second sentence. George Carlin's line saves the surprise until the very last word.

Each one of these jokes has a definite snap to it, just like the cracking of a whip. It's sudden, it's sharp, and it gets your attention. It tells the audience when to laugh. That's one of the major elements of a good joke. That's the *punch* in the punch line.

Listen for that kind of snap in your jokes as you review your routine while sitting in your own audience. If it's not there for each joke, try to put it there. When you're done, you'll have a funny, exciting monologue.

9
HOW TO WORK WITH WRITERS

As a writer on a Bob Hope special, I sat in on the table-reading of the script. That's a first reading where the performers sit around a table and read through the sketches and routines just to familiarize themselves with them and to hear them spoken aloud.

During this particular reading, Bob Hope turned to me after one joke and said, "Let's get a new punch line there. This one doesn't work." I immediately ad-libbed a replacement. Hope rejected it. I tried another one. He shook his head again. I tried a third. Hope said, "Gene, when we do a joke on my show, I like people to have some idea of what the hell we're talking about."

I knew he was kidding, but I went along with the joke. I threw my pencil across the room, slammed my script down on the floor and said, "Bob, now you're getting into more expensive comedy."

My favorite comedy-writer tale, though, involved the late radio comedian Fred Allen. The story has it that when Allen showed up at the studios one day, he overheard another star berating his writer for a poor script. The star cussed and fussed and yelled.

Fred Allen said to him, "Where were you when these pages were blank?"

These tales illustrate two important concepts to remember when working with comedy writers.

The first is that writers do expect and deserve to be paid. If you want material, you pay for it. If you want top-drawer material, you pay top price for it.

When I first started as a comedy writer, I was the comedy equivalent of an ambulance chaser. I would go to the clubs in my hometown, call the comics I saw perform, and offer them material. One gentleman I called was interested in new material, so he invited me to see him perform at the club where he was working.

I arrived before showtime so we could have a chance to talk. We sat at the bar and each of us ordered a drink. When the bartender presented the drinks, my comedian friend had vanished. I didn't know where he went; he was just gone. So I paid for the two drinks. As I counted my change, he reappeared.

We talked for awhile about what kind of material he wanted, when he needed it, and so forth. The bartender noticed our drinks were low. He offered a refill and we accepted. Again, when the drinks arrived, my friend was gone. I paid for the second round, and he materialized again.

This went on throughout the evening.

After the show, we talked again. He told me where he had purchased his tuxedo and how they had stylized it for him—piping along the lapels and some other embellishments. We were interrupted a few times with friends of his arranging golf matches. He would play with someone tomorrow, and he had another game arranged for Saturday, and one for Sunday. Through all this, we talked more seriously about my writing for him. When I asked about payment, he pleaded poverty. Things were tight right now, but if I could give him some good stuff and get him on "The Tonight Show," he'd send me a check.

I settled my bar bill (and his) and left.

This comic wasn't unusual. He boasted about how

much his fancy tux cost, and I know the tailor didn't furnish the cloth, do the stitching, and fit the suit on the basis that he would be paid if the comedian got on "The Tonight Show." Golf is not an inexpensive game and they don't advertise "Play now, pay later."

The gentleman had money for those things, but he didn't want to pay for comedy material.

And this is not limited to the weekend comic. Stars think the same about writers. Many times I would have high-priced stars come into my office with a plea. "I'm invited to a banquet tonight honoring the governor and I know they're going to ask me to say a few things. Could you write up a quick routine for me? I'll need it by tonight."

This request is never accompanied by any query about how much this would cost. They've never offered any payment. In fact, they've never even said, "Have lunch on me."

The writer's talent to them is expendable. It's not worth anything. I've often wondered what would happen if I reversed this situation. If I said to one of them, "Listen, my kids are having a party at their high school. I was wondering if you would stop by and do a few jokes about their teachers and maybe sing a song?"

If you are a comic, comedy material is valuable to you. The people who can create that material are important. Their work has value. You should recognize from the beginning that both you and they are professionals and all of your dealings should be on a professional level.

Second, comedy writers are not miracle workers. They're not fairy godmothers who can wave a magic wand and transform you into an hilarious stand-up performer.

All of your material has to be worked and reworked. It has to be broken in, polished, refined. Rarely will material roll out of the typewriter and go directly into your act as is. Both you and the writer have to agonize over the material, think about it, rethink it, rearrange it. Only then does it become a reliable, funny, strong piece of material good enough for your act.

Comedy writers are talented, creative people who can provide funny material for your act. If they do their job well, you should get good value for whatever you pay them.

With those thoughts in mind, let's investigate how you should work with writers.

Where Do You Find Writers?

Comedy writers usually aren't listed in the yellow pages. Finding the writer who can help your comedy presentations requires some detective work. You'll have to do some research.

I've always found with this kind of investigation that one clue always leads to another. You follow one lead and it leads to two or three other sources. Soon you're overwhelmed with information.

To give you an example, a few years ago I became interested in the speaking circuit. A librarian uncovered a newsletter on the speaking profession for me. I wrote to the editor, explaining that I was trying to learn more about this business. She sent me samples of her publication and recommended a speaker who had similar credentials to mine and was very successful as the kind of speaker I wanted to be.

I called this gentleman and he invited me to visit at his home for a weekend. He taught me a tremendous amount about speaking and the business of speaking.

He suggested that I join an association for speakers. I did. Through that organization, I met many other speakers, booking agents, and publicity people who were willing to exchange ideas with me.

The base of information continued to expand, and today I have a fairly successful speaking career that brings me to many places, earns me a little bit of money, and is an interesting sideline to my comedy-writing profession.

You'll experience the same phenomenon when you begin your search for competent writers.

Start at the library.

Find out if there are any organizations that deal with comedy and comedy writing and what magazines, newspapers, and newsletters are currently published on these subjects.

Then call or write for further information, membership requirements, or sample issues. Phone calls always seem more useful to me because they're faster and information is exchanged more easily. With a letter you ask one or two questions and the response answers those. With phone dialogue, the answers may prompt other questions on your part which can immediately be answered.

The Writers Guild of America is an association of television and screen writers. They have a West branch in Los Angeles and an East branch in New York City. The Guild publishes a periodical and also has a directory of members along with their writing credits.

There is also a Professional Comedians Association based in New York City and a Comedy Writers/Performers Association in Brooklyn.

Dramalogue is a periodical that deals with performing arts. *Just for Laughs* is a newsletter published for and about stand-up comedians. There is also a *Comedy USA Guide* that lists information about comedy performers and writers.

I'll let you do the research to find these and other organizations and newsletters. First, because doing your own research will help you to uncover other leads. Second, because addresses and phone numbers change. What I list in this book today may not be current by the time you read it. If you look up the addresses and phone numbers, you're more likely to get ones that are up-to-date.

I also help publish a newsletter for comedy writers and performers that I know you'll find helpful. It's called *Gene Perret's Round Table*, and our offices are in San Marino, California, outside Los Angeles.

There are also national and local writing clubs and associations that are not strictly related to comedy writing, but which might include humor writers.

Check the ads in trade papers.

Many times we skim over those classified and personal ads in the back of the periodicals we read. Now that you're searching in earnest for writers or ways to contact writers, it will be worth a quick read through these ads because you might find some useful information or contacts.

You could also place an ad in any magazines, periodicals, or newspapers that deal with comedy performing, comedy writing, or writing in general. Usually, the classifieds or the personals are inexpensive and can bring results.

You might also write a letter to these publications. In our newsletter, *Round Table*, we don't accept any paid advertising, but we often run letters from people who are looking for comedy writers. It's a way of furnishing marketing information to our readers. Many magazines and newsletters will do the same.

Ask other comedians about writers.

Do these comics buy material? Who do they buy from? Do they know of any writers who are looking for work?

Ask writers. Often I'm offered assignments or opportunities that I can't accept. Sometimes I'm too busy, I'm booked during that time, or I'm contractually prohibited from accepting another engagement. However, I always know of someone else who could handle the job.

It reminds me of the time some people approached a well-known comedian I worked for after his performance. They said, "We'd like you to be our Man of the Year. The membership overwhelmingly voted for you because of your outstanding contributions to the industry and to humanity in general. You are the person they want; you're the person they demand. You are the only person who truly has the qualifications to be our Man of the Year. We're holding the banquet and the Man of the Year presentation in Los Angeles on February 7th."

The entertainer said, "I'm sorry, but I'm booked all through the month of February. There's no way I could make it."

The representative said, "Oh, that's too bad. Do you know anyone else who could be our Man of the Year?"

Writers can usually lead you to a writing friend or several writing friends of theirs.

Let everyone know that you're looking for writers.

Tell your friends, your colleagues at work, your family, strangers you meet—everyone. It's a form of networking that can produce interesting and beneficial results.

People like to play matchmaker. They like to put you in touch with someone because it proves they know someone.

One of my first writing assignments came about through this sort of networking. I told people I worked with that I was interested in writing for comedians. One friend's father was a former musician who played for local entertainers. He talked to some friends of his who were still in the music business. They talked to one of the comedians who was on a nightclub bill with them. He said he'd meet with me as a favor. I met him, did some freelance work for him, and he introduced me to the host of a TV show that he guested on. That television host asked to see some of my comedy, so I sent a few samples. Later a comedian guested on the show, saw my material, liked it, called me, and we signed a contract. I worked for him for about seven years.

How Do You Find the Right Writers?

Some comedy writers have particular skills and outlooks that enable them to write for one comedian but not for another. Like every other profession, they specialize. You wouldn't insist that your podiatrist perform your heart surgery. No, you want a qualified thoracic surgeon to do that.

In your search for a comedy writer, you don't just want a comedy writer, you want a comedy writer who can produce material that *you* can use. The fact that someone has twenty years of experience, four Emmies, and has written for some of the top names in the business doesn't guarantee that person can write for you.

How do you find out if they can? You audition them. Ask interested writers to send you some sample material. If everything they send fits perfectly into your style, your sense of humor, and your act, then begin negotiating with them. You've found a gem.

If everything they send you is totally different from your style of comedy, you might have to look around some more.

I say "might" because you have to be sure that this writer knows what you want, what you're looking for. A comedian once called me and asked me to write some material for a convention he was appearing at. He told me it was a psychiatrist's convention, so I wrote a batch of appropriate jokes.

When I asked him how it went, he said, "Oh, I was wrong. It was a chiropractors' convention." I wrote good jokes, but he couldn't use any of them.

You have to make sure that the auditioning writers know exactly what style of routine you're looking for and what type of jokes. If that's made clear and their material still doesn't thrill you, there's no point in working with these writers.

One other point, though: Auditioning writers doesn't mean getting free material. If you decide that some of the submissions are worthwhile and you use them, you should pay for those at a fair price, even though you don't want to hire this particular writer.

Which brings us to the next question:

How Much Is This Going to Cost?

Well, how much is a house going to cost? How much is a car going to cost? A television? A vacation?

It depends, doesn't it? You have to decide what you want. You can get a nice fixer-upper that suits your needs for a reasonable price. You could also pay several million for an estate in Beverly Hills.

You can get a used Plymouth or a new Rolls-Royce. A portable black-and-white or a big-screen, high-intensity color TV. You can go to a bed and breakfast for the weekend or cruise the Caribbean for a month.

It depends on what you want.

Do you just want a few new jokes to keep your current act fresh? Then you might let a few writers know that you're in the market and that you're willing to pay $5 or $10 a joke for any that you buy.

Do you want a nice six-minute chunk to add to your act? Then you might have to find writers who can do that and pay them whatever their going rate is. It might be $1,000 to $2,500.

Do you want a dynamite song parody? Then again, you'll have to find the writers and pay their fee. It might be pretty steep.

Do you want someone who has talent, energy, creativity to help you develop your act? Do you want them to furnish topics, jokes, routines, criticism, and make sure that you're developing well as a comic? Then you're going to have to find someone special and put them on a retainer.

As we mentioned in the beginning of this chapter, you are going to have to pay if you hire writers. How much you pay and how you pay is negotiable. It depends on who you are, who they are, what you want, and what they want.

Let me give you examples of how two established stars worked quite differently from one another. Phyllis Diller would buy material from writers all over the country. She had a whole network of housewives writing her comedy. I know. I was one of those "housewives."

Back in the '60s, Phyllis would pay $5 for any joke she selected from your submissions. If a writer sent 100 jokes and Phyllis selected ten, she'd send a check for $50.

Phyllis was flooded with one-liners. People loved getting that check and boasting that they wrote for Phyllis Diller. Phyllis would stockpile these jokes, which were general in nature—about the things Phyllis did in her monologues—and pull from them anytime she wanted to update a routine or create a new one.

It was perfect for the writers and it worked well for Phyllis.

Bob Hope had different needs. He wanted top-drawer material immediately. He wanted fresh gags on headlines in the paper where the ink wasn't even dry yet. For that, he needed a stable of dependable writers. To be sure that these writers would work for him and were available when he needed them, he paid a top-dollar retainer.

Now let's look at those arrangements from the writers' points of view. Those who wrote for Diller were part-timers who were supplementing their income or aspiring writers who couldn't demand steady employment in the field yet. Phyllis represented either an extra so-many bucks a month or a stepping stone to the next phase of their careers. They were happy to turn out jokes whenever the spirit moved them and to submit them without the burden of particular assignments and demanding deadlines.

The Hope writers were professionals whose time was money. They had the credentials to land staff assignments.

They were proven, experienced writers who were used to high-paying assignments. If Hope wanted them, he had to pay them enough to justify their turning down other employment.

You can see from these two examples how much depended on who the comic was and who the writers were. Phyllis probably couldn't have convinced writers like those who worked for Hope to submit material for $5 a gag. Yet she got the quality and quantity she needed from the many writers who were willing to submit on that basis. Hope couldn't use writers unless they were available to work on demand, which Phyllis' writers weren't. Yet to get those writers, Hope had to pay on a different scale.

You have to decide what you need and which writers are able to and willing to provide that.

Once you know who you are and what you need and who they are and what they need, you can negotiate. You get what you need and give them what they need. It's usually money, but not always. And when it is money, how much is it and how is it paid?

When I was starting as a comedy writer, I wanted to take a correspondence course in writing jokes. I couldn't afford it. So, I went to several comedians who worked in my hometown and offered a deal. If they would pay for this correspondence course, I would give them all of the jokes that I wrote as homework assignments in the course. I got a comedian to give me the $150 I needed, I studied the course, and I sent my homework to the school and to this comic. He was happy, I was happy, and I presume the school was happy, too.

If you want the best jokes available from the most successful comedy writers in the business, you're going to have to pay top price for them.

However, you may be able to get fresh, innovative material from aspiring writers for a fraction of that cost. Most beginning writers need an outlet and some experience. You can offer them this (along with some cash) if they'll write for you.

They get to sell some jokes. They get to work along with a comic. They get to see their material in front of an audience.

As a free-lance comedy writer, I've sold jokes to performers for $5 a gag, I've had weekly retainers, I've signed year-long contracts, and I've written for performers for five percent of their fee. Performers and I have even bartered—"If you write some gags for me, I'll be able to do such and such for you." I've been content with every contract I signed.

You can find writers who will work for so much a joke, so much a week, so much a page, so much a year—almost any sort of remuneration package you can conceive.

The keys: How much can you afford and what are the writers willing to do this work for? You have to have some idea of your writing budget. Is it $100 a week? $100 a month? $100 a year? Whatever it is, you have to decide.

Then you must find a writer who is willing to work within that budget. You're not going to steal any of Jay Leno's writers for $100 a month. But you may be able to find someone who is good enough to write for Leno but hasn't gotten the break yet.

If you find that writer through your auditioning, you have to convince that person that it's worthwhile working for you for $100 a month. (Remember, I'm just using that $100 figure arbitrarily. I'm not recommending that as a typical fee. You'll have to decide on your own realistic budget.) You might negotiate over the amount of work they do for you, perhaps a page of gags a week.

I advise beginning writers not to price themselves out of a job too early. They read about the inflated prices that Hollywood writers "claim" to get, and then the young writers wants a comparable fee. My advice to writers is to get into the business first. Get a track record before you start demanding exorbitant fees. I tell them that they should get enough to justify the work they put into the job. They shouldn't feel cheated or taken advantage of. The cash exchanged should be fair; the writer's fringe benefit is the experience and the credit gained.

Without giving specific prices, any more than I could for a house or a television set, finding a writer should only cost you as much as you can afford. You set a writing budget that you can live with, then you shop for a good writer who can do your type of material at the cost you can afford to pay. If you're creative in your negotiations, and fair, you should be able with some effort, research, and some creative input of your own to find those writers.

How Do You Work with Your Writing Staff?

When I worked on "The Carol Burnett Show" people used to ask what a typical writer's day was like. There wasn't one. No day was typical; no day was like another. Why? Because we had so many different areas to work on. Each day's schedule depended on what problems arose that day.

For instance, the writing staff had to create premises for upcoming shows and for scheduled guest stars. We had to write those sketches. We had to rewrite those sketches after notes. The writing staff also had to solve problems on the show currently being produced. If a scene wasn't working, or if a piece of business was needed, or if a performer wanted a new and better line, or if the sketch was running too long and had to be cut— any or all of these had to be attended to immediately.

The writing process never ended until the material was on tape. In fact, sometimes it didn't end even then. Occasionally, we'd make additional edits in the material or write new jokes to be added to the soundtrack.

On television, the writing had to end sometime. When the show aired, it was finalized. We couldn't change things that were in the past tense, even if many times we wished we could. But a stand-up comic's routines are always changeable. They can always be improved. The editing process can go on forever and probably should.

The best possible arrangement you can have with a dependable writer whose talent and judgment you trust is a continuing working relationship. The writer should not only supply premises and gags, but also editorial comments and suggestions for polishing and refining your routines.

A good comedy routine is generally not born to full maturity. It needs care and nurturing until it develops and grows into a full-grown, solid, dependable piece of material. A good writer should be part of that development.

Most writers would prefer to be part of the material they create. They generally want to edit, rewrite, and polish their material until it's fine-tuned, almost perfect.

Once, my partner and I wanted to work on a certain television variety special, but we had a conflicting gig. Instead, we submitted some sketches that we had written previously.

When the sketches aired, we were disappointed. We saw flaws that we felt we could have corrected, improvements we might have made. It's no fun for a writer to feel barred from the ongoing creative process.

I recommend finding a writer, through auditions, who you feel has both the talent and the personality to work with you on your comedy. Invite that writer to see your act, or at least send a tape so that he or she can hear your act.

Watching you perform, a writer gets a better feel for your style and delivery. If a writer is going to write for you, he or she should know what kind of performer you are.

That writer should note your strengths and weaknesses and the powerful and weak parts of your act.

The writer can also be a spy in your audience. While you're performing, the writer will be aware of the listeners' reactions. The writer then has a better knowledge of which types of material are your most effective.

Then have that writer suggest some premises that you approve, and write those pieces.

Together, you prepare the pieces for presentation. Make cuts, changes, additions until you feel it's ready for presentation, remembering all the time that you are the driving force behind this piece of material. You're the one who has to stand before an audience and present it, so you make the executive decisions. You tell the writer where you want changes and how you want the piece improved.

I recall one time when Bob Hope pointed out a joke in the script and told me to get a new gag to replace it. I thought the joke was funny, so I said, "What do you want a new line for?" He said, "Laughs."

Finally, you can direct the writer in polishing and refining the material once it's before the audience. You'll know which lines are weak, which sections are slow. You direct the writer's efforts to repair those sections.

With this modus operandi, you're constantly updating your act, improving it. You and your associate are keeping an eye on your performances and maintaining them. You're also keeping the writer involved in the act. He or she doesn't just zip something through the typewriter and then forget about it. That writer, with you, is committed to making that material work and keeping it working well.

That's really what you want and expect from a writer. It's what you're paying for.

Of course, in all of the above I've referred to "the writer" almost as they do in legal documents. If you can afford two, three, four, or ten writers, all the better.

One final caution in working with writers: They have egos that bruise easily. It's to your benefit to keep their creative juices flowing. The more inspired they are, the more productive they'll be. The more their egos are fed, the more the quality of their work will improve.

One time I was free-lancing for two comedians. I sent both of them a batch of thirty to forty jokes. One called up and berated me over the phone. In all of that material, there were only two jokes that were getting any response at all. He was upset because he paid for all those jokes and only two were working.

I hung up hating this guy and feeling that he offended me and my talent. I wrote more lines for him, but I don't think my heart was in it.

The other comedian called up and was ecstatic with the material I sent. "Hey, man, two of those jokes you sent are getting giant laughs and applause from the audience. They love them. What I want you to do is try to write a few more gags like those on the same topic, Okay?"

Sure it was okay. I immediately sat down and banged out some inspired work and sent it to him. We worked together for several years.

What was the difference? Each one got only two gags out of a batch of about thirty-five—not a great batting average. However, one comic saw the potential in the routine and prodded me to write more and better material. The other guy just turned off any creative flow that I might have had going.

So, in working with writers, remember Fred Allen's admonition. "Where were you when the pages were blank?" Part of your job as the writer's employer is to keep that person's energy up. Keep your writer inspired. I guarantee you'll get more for your money that way.

10
BE FUNNY, NOT JUST DIRTY

Okay, this is the chapter where I might lose a few disciples. I'm unabashedly in favor of clean material, especially for beginning comics. At a seminar that I host each year in Palm Springs for comedy writers and performers, we have Mike Night. That's an evening in which we all enjoy dinner followed by performances of any of those participants who want to show off their comedy act.

As host, I set a few rules. One is a strict time limit because we sometimes have so many acts that if we allow performers to run over, we'll be there until three in the morning. Besides, it's good training to be able to trim your act to rigid time restrictions. It's what television demands. The other is that the act be clean.

Naturally, I get flak on both scores. "My act is so compact, and so perfected, that if I cut even twenty seconds it won't be as effective." My response: If you were invited to do the Jay Leno show and Leno demanded that you cut twenty seconds or not do the show, you'd cut the twenty seconds, wouldn't you? All of our comedians trim their acts and finish on time.

The biggest grumbling, though, is over the "clean act" requirement. My response: Television demands clean material, too.

Most of our performers adjust their act and usually benefit from it. Some have surprised themselves when they discover that they can get good audience response with the questionable material filtered out. In some cases, they realized that their act became stronger.

So, at our Mike Night, we continue to suggest that performers do clean comedy. I'm offering the same advice to you through this book. Understand, though, that my recommendation is not prompted by prudery. Nor do I suggest it for moral, ethical, or religious reasons. It's business advice, pure and simple.

I don't mean to censor your act in any way, nor do I want to restrict the enjoyment of adults who want to go to a club and hear whatever kind of entertainment they want. My only goal is to make you a better and more successful stand-up comedian.

I know some comics who will say, "Screw everybody. I'm going to say what I want to say, and if they don't like it, that's their tough luck." Well, that's a bold philosophy, but is it really their tough luck or is it yours? You're the one who wants to make a go of the stand-up business. You're the one who wants to become rich and famous. If your material keeps you from those goals, then it's your tough luck.

Here's why I recommend a clean act, or at least enough clean material in your arsenal so that you could do a clean act.

Blue Material Cuts Down Your Potential Audience.

You're a funny performer. I love the comedy you do and I can't wait to tell my friends about your routines. In fact, I want to see you the next time you're in town and I want to bring some of my friends to see you. I want to bring my family to see you. I want to bring my kids . . . well, wait a minute. Maybe I shouldn't bring the kids. In fact, some members of my family might not like some of your routines. A few of my friends might object, too.

Do you see what's happening? You're an up-and-coming comic. You want your reputation to spread. Why inhibit it? Why limit your appeal?

Your response may be that you're an adult comedian. You do and say what you want, regardless of how offensive it may be to some. Fine, then you will attract only "your crowd."

My question: Why limit yourself? If you're genuinely funny and creative enough to analyze any subject and extract humor from it, why not entertain everyone?

Consider those comedians who have general appeal—Bill Cosby, Steve Martin, Jerry Seinfeld. Wouldn't they be unwise to introduce offensive material into their act that would alienate half of their audience? They have the right to do it. They have that freedom. But why?

That's after the fact. You have that choice before the fact. You can gather fans from a wide universe, why limit yourself now?

Blue Material Limits Your Marketability.

Several people in the movie industry campaigned a few years ago for an intermediate adult rating. There is nothing between an "R" rating and an "X" rating, they argued. The "R" meant that anyone under the age of seventeen had to be accompanied by an adult. The "X" meant that no one under twenty-one would be admitted. Besides, the "X" generally signified pornography.

The campaigners insisted that there could be some themes and scenes that were more powerful than the "R" but not necessarily pornographic. Eventually, they won a new rating, "NC-17." This means no one under seventeen will be admitted.

Now the producers struggle to avoid the "NC-17" rating. They feud with the rating board when a picture is given the "NC-17" rating. Reluctantly, they'll snip scenes from films in order to have them reduced to an "R" rating. Why? Money.

Many newspapers have a policy that refuses to carry advertisements for "NC-17" and "X" films. Some theatre chains will not show "NC-17" films. Consequently, the movie gets less publicity and less exposure to the audience. The result is that it makes less money.

You, as a budding stand-up comic, have the same dilemma, although not so rigidly rated. You acquire a reputation for the material you do and the type of act you present. This affects your marketability.

The people who book the comedy clubs have their own standards of propriety. Some will allow practically anything. Others have a line that they will not cross. Some, like my annual seminar, are strict.

As an aspiring comedian, this is your marketplace. These are the people who have the power to put you onstage. They hold your career growth in their hands. Why dismiss a goodly percentage of them?

Isn't it better to be able to say to them that you can deliver whatever sort of act they require? "Do you want funny? I got it." "Do you want funny and clean? I got that, too." Doesn't that sound like better business?

I've spoken to several comedy-club proprietors, and most of them prefer the comics who can be funny and clean. Why? Again, money. They want their clubs filled every night. The more people who are in their room, the more money they make. So why would they adopt a policy that would limit the audience?

Then why do so many of them have comics who are borderline? Because they can't find enough who can be funny and clean. There's a need for that kind of comic. Again, appealing to your business sense, it's wise when you find a need like that to fill it.

Valhalla for a stand-up comedian is television. You've arrived when you can land a guest spot on "The Tonight Show" or a short chat next to David Letterman. That's proof that you're at the top of the comedy-club circuit, and it can often be the springboard to more exposure and even greater riches. You might become a regular guest on television shows, or you could even land your own sitcom like Gabe Kaplan, Freddie Prinze, Jerry Seinfeld, and Roseanne Arnold did. Now you're making real money.

However, network television won't let you perform blue material. They will censor your act. If you want to guest with Jay Leno, you have to have six to ten minutes of "television clean" material. Here's the catch, though: If you want to impress the TV world, it has to be solid material. There's no point in guesting on the show with a permissible routine that's only fair. You want to knock everybody's socks off.

You don't get that kind of material by being invited to guest on the show and then sitting down and writing it two days before your appearance. You have to create it, polish it, refine it, add and subtract from it. You have to be doing it all along in order to make it a solid routine.

Besides, if booking agents don't see worthwhile television material in your performances, you won't be invited to appear in the first place.

Several years ago, I went with the producers of a new variety show to a comedy club in Hollywood to audition talent. The club did a special show for us in which they featured most of their regulars at that time. We sat for three hours and listened to established acts. Only one had material that could be used on television.

We were there to buy comedy. We wanted and needed performers. They took themselves out of the marketplace with unacceptable material.

You might ask: Couldn't we recognize potential and realize that some of these performers might have made it with freshly written, television material? Perhaps, but we would ask in return: Couldn't these performers recognize their own potential and develop fresh, television-acceptable material? If they had confidence in their ability, why should we have to do their work for them?

That's what I'm saying to you—recognize your own potential and develop some material that you can depend on when an opportunity arises.

Blue Material Limits Your Creativity.

Comedians like Jerry Seinfeld and Rita Rudner amaze me. They can find humor in the most mundane, everyday things. Seinfeld can turn a walk through a supermarket into a sharp, funny chunk of material. Rita Rudner had hilarious routines as a single girl on the dating scene. Now, as a married woman, she can extract just as much fun and deliver it to her audiences. Steven Wright can do jokes about things that most of us would never even think about.

There's comedy in practically everything. The humorist's job is to find it, mine it, refine it, polish it, and present it to the listeners as a semi-precious commodity.

Part of humor is that unexpected exposure of something that you've seen every day and never quite noticed. It's presenting the ordinary in an extraordinary light. To do that effectively, you must comb through the ordinary for those comedy gems.

If you confine your search to the blue areas, you eliminate many sources of potential humor.

Blue Material Stunts Your Comedic Growth.

Shelly Berman did a question-and-answer routine once many years ago. I still remember one part of it. Someone asked, "What do you do when children ask where they came from?" Berman replied, "I've had good success with pointing."

I've since seen many comedians who've also had good success with pointing. A heckler shouted something from the audience, the comic pointed to his crotch. He told a joke that didn't work, he pointed to his crotch. He flubbed a line, he pointed to his crotch. Anytime he was stuck for what to do next, he pointed to his crotch.

Shelly Berman's line got laughs, and so did many of the comic's crotch pointings. Berman's line, though, was different—it was creative, it was funny. Pointing to the crotch is just pointing to the crotch.

However, pointing to the crotch was a crutch. The pun there might have been intended. That's one of the problems with blue material—it's easy.

I can remember being with the guys I used to hang out with. We'd get into laughing fits where everything we said sounded dirty and funny. It didn't matter what anybody said. To us it sounded filthy, and the filthier it sounded, the funnier it seemed. "I'm having trouble with my carburetor." "Yeah, that's what his girlfriend said—she didn't like his carburetor." Gales of laughter. What could be easier? Just say a big word with a bit of a leer and all your friends would think it was side-splittingly funny.

That same phenomenon can happen with comics. Why be clever? Why be inventive? Why be creative? Just say something off-color, or point to your crotch, and you get screams.

To grow as a comedian, you have to get better and better. Your material has to grow along with you. If you accept the blue material as your best, you're not going to develop comedically.

You're stunting your own growth.

I've heard all the arguments against my advice, too. Here are a few of them along with my responses.

But That's What People Want to Hear.

Are you sure of that? I travel around the country giving banquet speeches and lectures on humor. Often the talk is followed by a question-and-answer period. One question I get at every stop: Why is there so much blue material in comedy?

Many people don't want to hear it.

In fact, when I began as a comedy writer, I would sit in the audience and listen to some of my clients perform, then I would mingle with people after the show and gather their candid responses. They didn't know I was an associate of the performer. The one comment I heard most often was, "He was not only funny, but he was clean."

Many people prefer that.

Even comedians notice when a newcomer is funny without being offensive. They're certainly not censoring or being prudish, but they do recognize that the clean material usually indicates that this comic can be funny and inventive on any subject.

So, don't be too sure that that's what people want to hear.

But That's the Way People Talk.

It's realistic. That may be true, but artists are not supposed to present exactly what people say and do. A playwright condenses what people say into a compact form. He or she distills the essence of their speech into a play that holds the audience's interest. If they wrote what people actually say, the play would not only be boring, it would be redundant and would take about seventeen hours to perform.

I once had an editor criticize my writing because I used one particular word three times on the same page. In explaining to me why this was poor technique, he used the same word about fifteen times in one paragraph. People speak with poor grammar and improper technique, but writers shouldn't write the way people speak. They should write as accomplished artists.

Comedians don't have to echo the way people speak on the street. If they did, we wouldn't have to go to clubs to hear them; we could just stand on street corners. The comedian speaks in his or her own voice, not the way everybody else speaks.

Some classic films were made before speech was so liberated in movies. *Casablanca* was pretty effective without speaking the way people speak. So was *Gone With the Wind*, even if Clark Gable did have to resort to that one moment of weakness when he said "damn."

Jackie Mason once guested with Johnny Carson. Commenting about Hollywood, he noted that every movie he went to had a sex scene in it. For some reason or another, they had to show people naked. Jackie Mason wondered why this was so. When he questioned it, people told him, "That's what people do." Jackie Mason said, "People eat soup, too, but I don't see a bowl of soup in every movie."

Just because people talk that way is not an excuse for you to talk that way behind the microphone. It's rather a reason why you shouldn't. Your act should be set apart from that of everybody else, from the way people talk.

But Everybody's Doing It.

I used to try to pull that scam on my mother when I was a kid. "But Mom, Jimmy's mother is letting him do it." Mom would say, "If Jimmy's mother let him jump off the Brooklyn Bridge, would you jump with him?"

Mothers were unbearable when they got realistically logical.

While I'm writing this, the American economy is supposed to be bad. People can't find work and can't earn enough to support their lifestyle when they can. The average citizen is suffering. Does this mean that you should suffer, too? Does it mean that if you get offered a lucrative contract you should refuse it? You should suffer because "everybody's doing it"?

Besides, the fact that everybody's doing it should be the incentive you need not to do it. As a comedian, you want to be different, original, unique. You don't get to be that by doing what everybody else in the industry is doing.

How Do You Explain Eddie Murphy?

Eddie Murphy doesn't shy away from four-letter words and doesn't stick with television-clean material, yet he makes $15 million a year. How about that?

Eddie Murphy didn't make his name with blue material. He first gained prominence as a regular on "Saturday Night Live," a television show that sometimes skated on thin censorial ice. By definition, though, the material had to be television clean.

Also, Eddie Murphy is not a prominent stand-up comedian. He's an actor. He's worth $15 million per year because his movies do well at the box office, not because people are flocking to see his stand-up routines in the clubs.

So he's not a real role model for the aspiring stand-up comic.

Look rather to those comics who have made it through their stand-up routines into high-paying careers—Jay Leno, David Letterman, Jerry Seinfeld, Roseanne Arnold, Gary Shandling, Richard Lewis, Tim Allen, and others. Most of them did it with "television-clean" material.

If you think of many of the comedians who have become highly successful, you'll find that most of them did it with clean material.

It just seems to be the wiser choice.

Part Three

Your Delivery

11

REHEARSE YOUR ACT

When I was a kid in boarding school, the director assigned me to the school painting crew. I didn't particularly care for this duty because it meant plastering and painting ceilings. The ceilings in this school were high and I was unsteady with heights. I was afraid of them.

I spoke with the director and begged for a different chore, but he was indifferent to my pleas. So I painted ceilings.

Not my first day on the job, though. I climbed the ladders but still couldn't reach the ceilings. I was too frightened to stand on the scaffolding. From a sitting position I wasn't a very productive painter.

Gradually, I worked up enough courage to stand, grab hold of something, and paint the ceiling—very tentatively.

Within a remarkably short time, though, I was scrambling up and down the ladders, moving back and forth along the scaffolding, and reaching out precariously to get my job done as quickly and as well as I could.

I became sure-footed, steady, almost heroic high above the ground. How? Simply by doing it day after day, over and over again.

What is rehearsal? It's doing it over and over again. It's doing something so often that it becomes second nature to you. You do it almost unconsciously.

I've just taken up golf and am overwhelmed with the

mechanics of a good golf swing. You have to stand with your feet in a prescribed position with the ball located a given distance from your body and so many inches behind your left heel. The hands have to hold the club in a precise way, and the left arm must make a direct line from the shoulder through the club to the ball. The knees, hips, and shoulders must turn in a pre-ordained sequence to begin the backswing. At the top of the backswing, the club should be aligned with the ground and the target line in an unvarying fashion. Then the club, hands, shoulders, hips, and knees must begin the downswing with a strict regimen, striking the ball at the precise spot and following through as dictated.

When I stand up there to hit the silly thing, I have to remember as much of that as I can and tell my body and golf club to do it all. Yet a professional golfer told me once that the only thing he thinks about is to keep his chin pointed behind the ball throughout the entire swing. His hands, hips, knees, shoulders, club? He doesn't think about them through the swing at all. They automatically do what they're supposed to do. Why? Because through practice (the athletic equivalent of rehearsal) his body remembers each precise move it is supposed to make. And it makes them.

I guarantee this golfer's shots fly straighter than mine do.

You witness this same phenomenon in your daily life. Each time you get into your car, you most likely go through a very precise routine without being conscious of it. You probably open your door, get into the car and shut the door with the same moves each time you do it. You can talk to other people and think about different things, yet you go through several fairly complicated moves with unvarying precision.

Some performers may object. They argue that comedy is supposed to be fresh, new, original. It's supposed to have an element of surprise. True, but that's for the audience, not you. You're supposed to know what you're doing when you get onstage and be able to do it well.

Besides, rehearsal often brings out the nuances of the comedy material and enables the performers to discover little surprises in the script and in the way they deliver it.

I've sat in at hundreds of table-readings of scripts. I'm always astounded at how well experienced actors can deliver lines even when reading through them for the first time with other actors. Yet, as good as that first reading is, it's always flat when compared to the first run-through after two days of rehearsal and to the finished performance three days after that.

The performers find intonations, inflections, gestures, and pieces of business that enhance the comedy. It seems that each time they do it—each time they rehearse it—they learn something new. They can try variations and either keep them in or drop them, depending on how it helps the script and their delivery.

No actor would want to present to the public that first cold reading. In fact, those table-readings are usually opened only to the creative staff for that very reason. This is unrehearsed. This is unpolished. It's almost "unprofessional." So the actors don't want anyone there who doesn't absolutely have to be there.

Some might argue that rehearsal makes your performance stale. When you start your car in the morning, do you feel stale? Would it make you a better driver if you opened your car and started each morning with an entirely new procedure—just in order to keep you fresh and bright? No. You get in your car and start the engine effectively and efficiently. You do it the best way you know how so that you can get it out of the driveway and on the road.

A few might claim that some of the professionals get by with no rehearsal; therefore, it's the thing to do. Well, good comedy always should appear fresh and spontaneous. The good performers make it appear that way. Again, that's for the audience, not the performer. But the appearance of being unrehearsed doesn't always mean that the performer hasn't rehearsed.

I've been around professional actors and comedians for over three decades, and I don't know of many who will perform without some rehearsal. Once I asked Lucille Ball if she would ad-lib a little banter with Bob Hope on one of our TV shows. She said, "No way, honey. I want to see a script." She told me about an experience she had many years ago when a performer invited her to come onstage with her during one of his appearances. "We'll just chatter back and forth," he said. Then she got onstage with nothing but good intentions, and he had his writers prepare some "ad-libs." He came off clever and funny; she came off tongue-tied.

We gave her a finished script.

There's a story that applies here. I won't vouch for its authenticity, but it makes a point whether it's true or not. Dustin Hoffman appeared in the film *Marathon Man* with Sir Laurence Olivier. In one pivotal scene, Olivier tortures Hoffman in order to get information from him.

When they shot the scene, the story says, Hoffman was having trouble remembering his lines. He apologized to Olivier and explained that he hadn't slept in two days. Olivier asked why, and Hoffman said that he wanted to look drained, washed out, and exhausted for this scene as if he had been through the agony that this scene called for. Olivier said, "Have you ever tried acting?"

I'll paraphrase Sir Laurence now and ask, "Have you ever tried rehearsal?"

Rehearsal is such an integral, traditional part of theatre that it almost seems illogical to have to justify it. With comedy, though, its necessity is not so apparent. Again, when comedy is performed well, it appears improvisational, off the top of the head. That's the illusion. Many comedians, in fact, don't want their writers to publicize themselves because they want the public to think that all of those lines happen spontaneously. They don't want people to know that those lines are thought-out before-hand—and by people other than the comic.

Nevertheless, when comedy is performed well, it's usually because it has been well-rehearsed. There are many benefits to rehearsal. Here are a few of them:

You'll Do Your Best.

I mentioned earlier that I began my professional writing career almost by accident. I had been writing comedy as a hobby for some time when people I worked with asked me to write a roast and emcee the banquet for our supervisor, who was retiring.

I agreed, even though I was always reluctant—well, I was scared, actually—to speak before an audience.

I wrote my thirty-joke routine and then rehearsed it before a mirror every night for a month. I'd read the jokes aloud time and time again. It got so that once I started a joke, the ending of it would trip out of my mouth without me even thinking about what those words were.

Nevertheless, I was still frightened. At the banquet, I didn't trust myself to remember the routine, so I brought the script with me to the microphone.

I began, and it went beautifully. The audience and the guest of honor liked the jokes and laughed appreciatively. I was thrilled and relieved.

A good friend of mine paid me a high compliment when he said, "Man, you surprised me. I thought for sure you were going to be lousy."

He bought me a congratulatory drink and then said, "You know what surprised me most? Your voice was real strong and you read each line perfectly, even though that piece of paper in your hand was shaking like crazy."

He was right. I was frightened and unsteady while I was at the microphone, yet the words came out confidently and well. Why? Because I had rehearsed them so long and diligently. Though my body was literally trembling, my voice continued on its own. It was well-rehearsed. It did its best.

Had I not been rehearsed, the nervousness would have won out. I would have tripped over phrases, spoken them haltingly, ruined solid punch lines. The time I spent before the mirror speaking the words aloud enabled me to do my best at the microphone.

There are often upsetting moments in show business. You've surely heard of "opening-night jitters." It's hard to take a show onstage for the first time without a few butterflies in your belly. Some have said that rehearsal doesn't eliminate the butterflies; it just gets them to fly in formation.

There are nights when for whatever reason—a big audition or someone important in the audience—you are concerned about doing well. You're tense, fidgety.

I've been with performers backstage who were upset almost to the point of being sick before their cue. Then they went onstage and belted out the song as if they didn't have a care in the world.

There are other distractions, too, not just nerves. You might have a heckler. You might be working in a club where the microphone is faulty or the lights aren't right. The clickety-clank of glasses and dishes as the patrons are being served can get to you. In fact, rarely do things go 100-percent perfect for any performance. Despite any or all of those disturbances, you want to be the best comedy performer you can be.

That's what rehearsal can do for you. It enables you to get out there and do the best possible job you can.

Rehearsal Enables You to Concentrate on Your Job.

It's irritating to be stuck behind student drivers. In fact, it's more than irritating; it's dangerous. You're never quite sure which direction they're going to go, when they're going to stop, or if they're going to stop. Other drivers behind you get impatient and may do something precarious to get past both you and the student.

The poor student drivers don't mean to cause hazardous conditions, but they do. Why? Because they are not yet well enough "rehearsed" in driving. They're so busy worrying about fundamentals and what to do inside the car that they're not aware of traffic conditions outside of the car. They're so concerned about *how* to drive safely that they're not driving safely.

An actor's job is not to move across the set on a certain line of dialogue and stop at exactly the right mark. It's not to say certain words of dialogue on cue. An actor's job is to act, to play a role with such emotion and believability as to convince an audience that that character is real. An actor must make an audience feel the power and the passion of the play.

Hitting the mark, knowing the lines, and being at the right spot on the stage at the right time are the tools that enable the actor to do the job. They're what knowing how to work the gas pedal, the gearshift, the turn signals are to the student driver.

By practicing, the beginning driver becomes accustomed to the mechanics of operating an automobile and then is free to worry about surrounding traffic and, consequently, drive better. By rehearsal, the actor learns the lines, memorizes the positions onstage, and responds to the cues of the other performers. Then that actor is able to devote energy to the real job—acting.

A magnificent actor cannot give a magnificent performance without knowing the lines, the crosses, and the cues. No one in the audience would believe the performance if the actor is wandering around the stage befuddled instead of emoting.

Rehearsal is essential to the performance.

Stand-up comedy is not reading clever lines and making funny faces and gestures. It's entertaining an audience. With rehearsal, you can concentrate on that and that alone. You'll say your funny lines and make your funny faces and gestures, but all of your thinking, all of your energy, all of your skill will be directed toward your audience, toward making them laugh.

By being well-rehearsed, you can give your full devotion to that, your real job.

Rehearsal Reduces Fear.

Years ago, I worked with a youngster who was going to participate in the "Punt, Pass & Kick" competition. This was a football contest in which the young athletes threw and kicked the ball and were scored for distance and accuracy.

The lad I helped was only eight years old, just old enough to qualify. He had never really played much football, so we practiced these skills. I would hold the ball and he would run up and kick it as far as he could. I'd have him throw the ball and try to hit a target a few yards away. The practice was fun because, after all, he was throwing and kicking a ball and running around the park.

I couldn't be with him on the day of the competition, but he came home with a first-place trophy for his age division. I believe I was more excited than he was. I said, "How did you manage to do so well?" He said, "When my turn came, I just pretended we were still at practice and I did real good."

As I mentioned earlier, there is fear in show business—opening-night jitters, stage fright, and so on. In fact, it might even be the fear that attracts some of us to the stage, much the same way the danger attracts some to race-car driving. It's exhilarating for some to face that challenge and come away a winner. It's exciting to walk onstage before a crowd of strangers and convert them to fans. But it's also frightening.

Fear can detract from a performance. Picture a length

of board about two feet wide and ten feet long. Could you safely walk across that? Of course you could. Now, though, picture that same board if it were suspended between two buildings thirty stories high. Could you walk across it now? If you had enough courage to attempt it, you'd probably walk uncertainly and with very short, shaky steps.

The board has the same physical dimensions and you have the same walking skills. The difference is fear. You're now frightened and it affects your performance.

The way to defeat fear is to do something often enough so that you know you can do it with confidence. Doing something often is rehearsal. Probably, you won't walk across a board suspended between two tall buildings often enough to become proficient at it. Why should you? You don't want to be a good "board walker between tall buildings." However, you *do* want to be a good stand-up comic.

So rehearse.

Rehearsal Helps You to Learn What You *Can't* Do.

Suppose you choreograph a great halftime entertainment show that's to be featured at the NBA All-Star Game. You want it to be dazzling, exciting, captivating. And it is. You've done a superb job.

In fact, you've got me starring in it. At our first rehearsal, I read the script, which calls for me to execute some exciting dance steps, do a few tricks with the sparkling gold basketball you've had designed for the show, and then dribble down toward the basket, leap up, and slam-dunk the ball.

I'm only five-foot-nine when I'm soaking wet and I have knees that abandoned their flexibility a few years ago. You and I are going to discover that there's no way I'm going to jump high enough to stuff the basketball. Even if you introduce a trampoline into the act to get me up high enough, I still have to come down.

I just can't do it. Our rehearsals will substantiate that.

I'm sorry to disillusion you, but there are certain things you can't do in your stand-up act, either. It's no insult; there are certain things all of us can't do. And I don't mean can't do well; I mean you just can't do them. Rehearsals should find those things for you. You can then eliminate them before you look foolish trying to do them before an audience.

Wouldn't I look dumb if the public-address announcer declares to the crowd that I'm going to dribble down and slam-dunk the ball and I only get two inches off the ground?

What kind of things can't you do? Some comics can do pantomime; others can't. Some can tell a story with facial expressions; others can't. Some can effectively do magic tricks; others can't. You can do some things that others can't, but you can't do some things that others can. How do you find out what you can and can't do? Rehearse.

Rehearsal Promotes Spontaneity.

A friend of mine collects oxymorons—jumbo shrimp, divorce court, and the like. Is this another one for his collection: rehearsed spontaneity?

Not really, because I'm not saying that the spontaneity itself is rehearsed, but that being well-rehearsed allows a performer to be more spontaneous.

Have you ever watched a youngster who is in the first year of piano lessons practicing a recital piece? The kid glares at the sheet music, her brow is furrowed. She's struggling to interpret the notes and at the same time get her fingers to move to the right keys. You don't dare speak to her while she's concentrating. If you did, she probably wouldn't hear you. She's lost in thought. She can't play and carry on a conversation at the same time.

Then you visit a cocktail bar and watch the pianist enjoy a drink, smoke a cigarette, kibitz with the customers, and try to make out with one or two of the unattached females, all while playing a swinging rendition of "I Get a Kick out of You."

If one of the patrons wants to sing along, he may say, "Can you play that in a lower key?" The piano player does an arpeggio that blends into a different key, all without missing a puff on his cigarette or taking his eyes off the unattached females.

The frustrated piano student has all she can do to play the notes that are written. She wouldn't even attempt any variations or key changes. She hasn't played enough yet to be familiar with all the nuances of music and the piano keyboard.

The professional, though, has rehearsed and practiced and played so long that he knows every key, every tempo, every song. He can improvise and create at the keyboard. His years of study and practice have given him that freedom, that flexibility.

A stand-up comic who is well-rehearsed has that same freedom onstage. He or she can experiment, improvise, leave the confines of the act to create fresh material or deal with specific situations, then return to the script.

When your style, your material, and your delivery are so well-rehearsed that they're second nature to you, you can be spontaneous at the microphone. It just might pay unexpected dividends.

12
"HOW ARE YOU?"

Early in my writing career, I did free-lance work for a fairly well known and successful stand-up comedian. Occasionally I would travel with him to watch him work and to do some work with him on the act. During one of these trips, an entrepreneur called and asked to have lunch with this comic. He had a business proposition that might earn the entertainer $1 million.

Even if you're skeptical, a $1 million offer is hard to resist, so my employer agreed to have lunch with this gentleman. I went along.

When the gentleman arrived, he looked like an entrepreneur. He had a nice suit, nice tie, and carried a very business-like briefcase. We shook hands and he got right down to business. He snapped open his briefcase, took out a few papers, and began. He said, "Er . . . uh . . ."

The comedian turned to me and said, "This guy's gonna make me $1 million and he starts with "Er . . . uh . . .?"

We live in a fast-paced world today. The mails were replaced with overnight deliveries and then by fax machines, which are almost instantaneous. We build faster highways and then travel on them at speeds that are illegally fast. We cook our meals in microwaves that take less than a minute, and we stand there tapping our foot waiting for them to be done. Steven Wright says that he has a microwave fireplace that allows him to sit in front of a roaring fire for the entire evening in only eight minutes.

We're in a hurry.

Writers who want to sell a book or a magazine article must first send a query letter to the publisher. The people who read these letters suggest that you get right to the point in the first paragraph. Grab the readers' attention quickly or they'll ignore the rest of the letter.

Magazine editors advise that the opening paragraph of any article you submit be one that seduces the readers. They want that first paragraph to grab and hold the readers, entice them to continue reading the article. If it doesn't, they don't want to publish your piece.

People who read speculative screenplays have told me that if they're not enthralled with the story within the first ten pages of a script, they'll abandon it. They'll toss it into the "return with a polite reply" stack and move onto the next submission.

Folks who go to bars to meet Mr. or Ms. Right always try to conceive that great opening line that's going to make the other person fall immediately in love with them.

Yet young comics still come onto the stage, grab the microphone, and say, "Hi . . . How are you? . . . Are you having a good time?"

It's the stand-up comedian's equivalent of "Er . . . uh . . ."

I suggest you walk to the microphone and hit them between the eyes with a great opening line. Knock them on their keesters. Grab the audience by the lapel and say, "Listen to me. I'm funny. If you don't pay attention, you're gonna miss some comedy gems."

"Hi . . . How are you?" is a waste of time—yours and theirs.

The late Godfrey Cambridge was an overweight black

comedian who gained prominence during the time of the Civil Rights movement. He had a startling opening line. He'd walk to the microphone and introduce himself saying, "My name is Godfrey Cambridge. I'm six-foot-two, and I weigh 185 pounds." That was obviously untrue. He continued, "Anybody who doesn't believe that is prejudiced." BAM! He had the audience hooked.

Max Alexander is a white, overweight comic who has a very effective opening line. Max works slowly and deliberately, but confidently. He doesn't have to rush because he's sure of his punch lines. He knows his gags will deliver laughs.

Max walks onstage and takes the mike from the stand, as hundreds of other comics do. He sets the mike stand upstage, again as many other comedians do. He says, "I'll move this out of your way. You'll be able to see me better."

BAM! He's got their interest.

One of my favorite opening bits is Dean Martin's. He comes onstage with a cigarette and a drink. He acknowledges the applause as he walks to center stage. He puffs on the cigarette and sips the drink as the applause gradually dies down.

He stands there for a bit looking at the audience. Then he walks over to his accompanist at the piano, leans over to him, and says, "How long have I been on?"

BAM! He's got solid laughter.

Those are all better than "Hi . . . How are you? . . . Are you having a good time?"

Some of you may wonder what is so disastrous about asking an audience how they're doing and if they're having a good time. It doesn't take more than a fraction of a minute.

The problem is that you've lost the opportunity to be different, to be unique, to stand out from the 99 out of 100 other beginning comedians who walk onstage and say "Hi . . . How are you? . . . Are you having a good time?"

This was your chance to tell this audience to look at you, pay attention to you, because you're funny. You're here to get laughs, you're here to entertain this crowd, and you take that responsibility seriously. This was your chance to say to this crowd, "We've got lots of fun coming up, so let's get right to it."

You want to open with that kind of impact. You want to hit them right between the eyes. BAM! You want to get their attention right at the start and hold it till the end of your set. "Hi . . . How are you?" doesn't do that for you.

It's dead time. It's like static on a radio.

There are no punch lines. There aren't even any lines that build to punch lines. It's simply "chuffa." "Chuffa" is a word that's used to denote the barely audible talk that extras would do on a movie or television set. The director doesn't want to hear any intelligible words, but he does want the hum of conversation in the background so the extras repeat the word "chuffa" over and over again.

When comics open with small talk, they might as well stand there and say into the microphone, "Chuffa, chuffa, chuffa, chuffa, chuffa, chuffa."

I asked Phyllis Diller about this once, and she agreed that comedians should open with a bang. Start with a laugh. She told me that's how she created the zany costumes that became her signature.

She said, "I wanted to start with a joke as soon as I reached the microphone, but I had nothing to joke about. So, I came up with these wacky looking costumes." She had wild colors, gold lamé dresses, feather costumes, a bit of everything. "The costumes themselves would usually get some chuckles," she says, "and then I'd always have a few jokes about what I was wearing."

She might wear a bright yellow dress with a very short

skirt and say, "Have you ever seen a chicken with funnier looking legs." Or she might wear a dress with great big oversized buttons down the front of it and say, "Don't laugh. If it weren't for these buttons, I'd have no shape at all."

Phyllis didn't want to know how the crowd was doing, where they were from, or if they were having a good time. She wanted a laugh. So she opened with a funny line.

For each costume that Phyllis had, she would try out several opening lines, listen to the audience reaction, and eventually use only the best.

You should begin building an opening that is just as sudden, just as sharp, and just as sure-fire. Here are a few of the benefits:

First, an effective opening gets the laughter started. Audience reaction is precarious. Every entertainer knows that you can lose an audience if you allow them to relax. The performer should always be in charge while onstage. Once he or she loses that control over an audience, it's often hard to regain it. The customers can be laughing like crazy, and then stop. Once they stop, it's sometimes difficult to get them started again.

If you open with "chuffa," you're letting them stop. In fact, you're forcing them to stop. You're distracting them from the entertainment with humdrum questions.

A good opening, though, keeps the audience in the show. It keeps the laughter rolling.

I worked with a comedian who told me a frightening tale of how his strong opening was thwarted. He said that other comics had always told him how difficult this one comedy room was. This gentleman was having pretty good success as a newcomer, but the veterans kept warning him about this "impossible" room. The crowds here were notoriously tough and cruel to scared newcomers. Like mad dogs, they sensed your fears, bared their fangs, and attacked. Those were the tales he heard.

"You'll die there," they said.

"No, I'll kill them there," he answered.

In spite of all the warnings, or more likely because of them, he sharpened his opening for this club. He was determined to start strong, capture this crowd, and deliver their heads to the people who were taunting him.

When he finally worked this particular club, his opening was dynamite. These people sat up and listened to this brash young comic who walked out on that stage and took charge. He was home free . . . he thought.

Then, suddenly, someone at ringside stood up, groaned, and collapsed onto the table. Others in the audience rushed to this person's aid. Instead of listening to this performer's jokes, the audience was now listening to shouts of "stand back . . . give him air."

Everyone's eyes were on this chaotic scene as the unfortunate's friends eventually carried him out of the club. No one knew if he was seriously ill, overcome by the room's atmosphere, or had had too much to drink. Whatever it was, the audience worried about it, wondered about it, and was no longer interested in the performer's monologue.

He stood at the microphone thinking, "Hey, remember me? The headliner? The guy you were just laughing at?" He finished his set, but no one really cared. He bombed. After such a beautiful, rewarding opening few minutes, he bombed.

It's a drastic way of losing a crowd, but it does make the point that audiences, even good audiences, can be lost. You might go through your entire professional career without having to deal with an emergency in the room— let's hope so, anyway.

But why create your own mini-emergency? Why stop the audience laughter? Why interrupt their concentration and their response with chuffa?

Second, a strong opening gets the listeners' attention. In a nightclub or a comedy club, if you allow the audience some free time, they're going to start conversations with their friends. They're going to begin doing their own comedy among themselves. They're not even going to hear you. You want to keep their attention focused on the stage, where you are.

In taping "The Carol Burnett Show," we would often have to stop taping for set changes, costume changes, whatever. Carol insisted that at least one of the stars be onstage during all of these breaks to talk to the audience. She wanted their attention riveted to the stage at all times, even when nothing was happening. She realized that if their minds wandered, they might not come back.

I used to watch the local fights from the Olympic Auditorium in Los Angeles every Thursday night. One big heavyweight knocked out his opponent in his first professional match. I forget the lad's name, but we'll call him Mike Drammer. He was tall and overweight for an athlete, but he must have delivered one helluva punch because it took only one to knock out his first opponent.

When he came into the ring for his second professional fight a few weeks later, he was all show. He wore red, white, and blue trunks and a large Uncle Sam-type hat. He danced around the ring as if he were the heavyweight champion. He billed himself now as Mike "Super Slammer" Drammer.

His opponent was just another heavyweight with normal boxing shorts and a robe. The referee gave the fighters their instructions at the center of the ring, and each returned to his corner. "Super Slammer" still played to the crowd.

The opening bell sounded, and while "Super Slammer" was still dancing and waving to the crowd, his opponent rushed over, hit him with a right cross, and knocked him senseless.

The referee counted "Super Slammer" out, and I never

saw him fight in that arena again.

The moral: When the fight starts, your attention should be on the fight. The opponent said to himself, "You're paying more attention to the crowd than you are to me, so I'm going to rush over there and get your attention." He did.

You must be just as ruthless. Once your name is announced, you're the center of attention. If the audience isn't giving you your due, you have to get it from them. You can do that with a powerful opening.

Third, an effective beginning labels you as funny. That's very beneficial, especially for a lesser-known comic. Some tension exists anytime a relative unknown comes center stage. There's a subliminal resentment in at least part of the audience. "How come you're up there with the spotlight on you and I'm down here at an undersized table buying overpriced drinks?" A smug "make me laugh" attitude permeates a percentage of the audience.

You're being challenged, and the longer it takes you to respond to that challenge, the more difficult it becomes for you to win.

Michael Caine tells in his autobiography, *What's It All About?*, how he first met and worked with Anthony Quinn. Caine says that rumors about Quinn preceded his appearance on the set. Crew members warned Michael that Quinn was a tough man, hard to get along with. At their first meeting, Quinn said he had heard that his co-star claimed to have come from a poor family. Caine said he did. Quinn said that the difference between a poor British family and poor Mexican family was considerable. He said to Michael Caine, "I don't think you really understand true poverty."

Caine said, "I have spent most of my life trying to avoid finding out."

Quinn laughed and said, "You and I are going to get on," and they did.

A good laugh can break the ice, and you know that there is often a thin layer of ice between the audience and an unknown comedian.

Fourth, a clever opening can win over people who are either skeptical or hostile. I worked in industry for thirteen years, and I learned that the toughest audience in the world was a group of employees listening to one of the top executives. We hated this guy's position and resented the fact that he was now going to chastise us, reprimand us, or warn us about some sort of impending corporate disaster.

It was always bad news and generally our fault, in the executive's opinion. The only time they invited the hoi polloi to an assembly was when it was bad news. If it were good news, all the top executives would be busy at some expensive dinner at a plush eatery congratulating one another on their managerial skills.

So there was a lot of ice when this executive took the microphone. Yet, a few of them won us over by having an honest, down-to-earth, amusing opening.

One gentleman, during low-profit times when many of the employees—and executives—were being laid off, began by saying, "I'm going to keep this mercifully short. I want to finish this while you and I are still working for this company."

We were still resentful of this executive's message, but we listened politely because he convinced us that he was Okay. He knew the score and was just doing his unpleasant corporate duty.

When I used to write free-lance comedy material for nightclub comics, I was always pleased and complemented when I would see conversions from my seat in the audience. I would eavesdrop on other tables, and often I'd hear guys trying to impress their dates with their pseudo-sophistication. They'd be determined not to laugh at this performer who "thinks he's funny."

Then the comic would open with a great line that would fracture the audience, including this sophisticate. I'd enjoy it as a mild sort of revenge.

But you have to convert these people fast and hard. The best place to do it is at the beginning of your act, with a fantastic opening line.

Fifth, a quick, snappy laugh saves you valuable time. You're onstage. You've struggled to get there and now you must make your impression—on the audience, the booker, your agent, whomever. You may not have that much time, either. The club owner wants you on and off in so many minutes.

Why waste time with "chuffa?" Get to the laughs. The sooner you get to the first one, the sooner you can get to the next one, and the next one, and the next.

Sixth, that first laugh lifts your spirits. Most of the time when a comedy-club comic asks, "How are you doing?" or, "Are you having a good time?" there are a few weak responses, but mostly apathy. It's disheartening.

But a laugh is energizing. It pumps you up. Earlier, in Chapter Three we talked about the synergism between the performer and the audience. This quick opening laugh will activate that.

Let's face it, when you walk onstage, you're a bit unsteady. You may be loaded with bravado, but there's a little corner of your soul that's frightened. Something inside you whispers, "God, I hope I go over tonight."

Why let that fear survive too long? Get your first laugh and dispel that anxiety. A quick laugh will make you perform better right away. You'll get the most from your material and the audience will get what they want from you—entertainment.

13
LET THEM HEAR YOUR
JOKES

A few years ago there was a gentleman, Al Kelly, who made his living from double-talk. Occasionally, he'd appear as a guest star on television shows—he did "Candid Camera" often—but mostly he'd be a speaker at banquets, but not as Al Kelly. At the banquet, he'd be billed as an expert on tax returns, as a government figure who would explain the new regulations that were just enacted, as the latest member of the corporate board of directors. Then he'd address the attendees and go into his specialty— double-talk.

Kelly was an expert at his craft. He'd speak intelligibly for a while and then throw in a word that the audience thought they understood, but not quite. As a tax expert he might say, "Ladies and gentlemen, these latest tax laws are really quite simple if you just remember two things about them—first of all that they are crasman, and secondly that they are designed for the crisson of other gleem."

Some of the audience would lean forward to hear better. They felt they almost understood him. Perhaps they just had to be a little bit closer to the speaker to understand what he just said. Others would look confused. Some would turn to their seat mates and ask, "What'd he just say." Still others would nod in agreement with him. Those are the frightening ones, the ones who understood him.

But Al Kelly would go on. He always went on because if he stopped for too long, people would catch on to the gag too early. He'd say, "Let's read over this together. If you'll just open up the felman drim to page 9."

People would look around for their "felman drim," whatever the hell that was. Kelly would explain what it was. "It should have been in with the colman of grike that you were handed as you came in the door."

That explains it.

Eventually, of course, people would realize that this was a put on, that Al Kelly was talking gibberish to them and they were straining to understand it.

Typing the dialogue on the page doesn't do justice to Kelly's timing and expertise. He carried off the scam with such panache that his gibberish seemed to make sense, but not quite. Kelly turned being misunderstood into an hilarious, entertaining act.

Generally, though, not being understood or not being heard at all destroys comedy. That's the first thing that performers check at rehearsal—the sound system. Every entertainer wants to be heard in every part of the room. It's especially important for stand-up comics. Even Al Kelly had to be heard to be appreciated. If the sound system was substandard, people would just assume they didn't understand anything he said because they couldn't understand anything anyone said. It would take the fun out of his performance.

Stand-up comics stand up in the first place because they've got some jokes to tell, some punch lines to deliver. Those punch lines become totally impotent if no one can hear them or understand them.

Punch lines are your bread and butter. They are what's going to make you rich and famous. You want people to hear them clearly, to laugh at them, to repeat them to their friends, to talk about them the next morning in the office. You definitely do not want them to turn to the other people at their table and say, "What'd she say?"

Al Kelly was a funny performer and he did his thing magnificently. People laughed at it. But when *you* tell a joke, you want your audience to hear and understand every word, every syllable. When you deliver the payoff line to "Why do firemen wear red suspenders?" you don't want the listeners to hear "To hold the clelbid of their clom."

Spoken communication can be more complicated than it seems, especially when it goes through an electronic amplification. You speak the words. They go into a microphone, through some wires, are amplified, and come out of a speaker. Then they go into the hearing system of the listener and eventually register on that listener's brain.

The microphone, wires, amplifiers, speakers, ears, or brains of the listener might be defective. That would affect the communication. However, you notice that it all begins with you speaking the words. If you don't say them clearly and loudly enough, then the mike, the wires, the amplifier, the speakers, the ears, and the brains won't get the message. You, the comic at the mike, start the process.

Obviously, as a stand-up comedian who survives by the spoken word, you want it to be heard. There are other reasons, though, why you want to speak clearly and project your voice. Here's what happens if you don't:

You Distract Your Audience.

You commit the cardinal sin of comedy—you step on your own laugh lines. Your reason for being onstage is to tell jokes, to deliver punch lines. You want your listeners concentrating on those lines. They are what are going to make you a star. You want folks to hear your set-up, watch your gestures, be attuned to your inflections, and appreciate your punch lines.

One comic I worked with stopped a taping and called the director down to the stage. The director had no idea what was wrong until the star asked him, "Why is this actor crossing from one side of the room to the other?"

The director explained that he was trying to get him in position for another shot.

The star said, "But he's crossing on my punch line."

The director said, "But we don't have time to have him get in position otherwise."

The star said, "When I'm delivering a punch line, nobody moves."

They restaged the camera angles.

This comedian knew that it was distracting to have movement on the stage while he was delivering an important line, a punch line.

Yet if you deliver a line that is hard to hear or understand, you're distracting your own audience. You've got them looking around to see if anyone else appears to be having trouble hearing. You've got them turning to one another and asking, "What'd he say?" You've got them repeating your punch lines to one another while you're trying to deliver your next line. You're stepping on laughs.

And it's your fault.

You Disappoint Your Audience.

People sense when a good raconteur is nearing the payoff of the story. They know when a good comic is building to the payoff. They get excited about it. They anticipate. Then they don't hear it. It's a let down.

Audiences are very forgiving, though. The first one or two times that happens, they'll blame themselves. They'll assume they're not hearing well enough or not paying attention. They'll try harder.

Eventually, though, if it happens often enough in your act, they'll realize that it's not their fault at all, but the comic's.

They'll not only blame you, they'll get annoyed at you. You're building them up for a fall with too many of your jokes. You'll lose this crowd.

The sad part is you may lose them with excellent material. You may have good, solid, funny routines, but you're not getting them across. Nevertheless, you'll lose them.

You Appear Insecure.

The people in your audience are paying to be there. There might an admission charge, a slight tip for the person who seats them, perhaps a larger tip if they insist on a better seat, and probably a two- or three-drink minimum. They're paying because they expect to be entertained—by you. They want you to come to the microphone and take charge of their evening's fun.

During your set, you're the boss. The people out front have given you permission to be in charge during that time. They're paying to have you in charge.

However, a person with that kind of power must speak with authority. You must be heard and heard clearly. If you mumble or fumble, your credibility is immediately suspect. They lose confidence in you and your performance suffers.

Remember the entrepreneur we talked about in the last chapter? The one who began his million-dollar presentation with "Er . . . uh?" He could have closed his briefcase and walked out after that opening because he lost all believability. He was done. He was finished.

You must appear self-assured when you step behind the microphone. The audience demands at least that from you. It's difficult to do, though, if your speech is tentative, if you can't be heard or understood.

You Appear Amateurish.

Audiences love to be hip. The crowd wants to back a winner and reject a loser. It's peer pressure.

I watched a news broadcast many years ago when the film *Last Tango in Paris* premièred. This was a controversial film because it contained sex scenes that were considered shocking at that time.

On a local newscast in Los Angeles, journalists interviewed several celebrities as they left the première showing of the movie. Most of them said that it was a very engrossing film. Whether that was a valid opinion or more of a stand against censorship I don't know, but the Hollywood community's consensus was that the movie was indeed worthwhile.

Then one journalist spoke to Groucho Marx. Groucho was quite old and showing signs of feebleness at this time. He was usually accompanied by a female companion, but she wasn't there when the journalist posed his question, "What did you think of this film?" Groucho, in his inimitable outspoken style, said, "I thought it was terrible. I hated it."

His companion, who was talking with other theatregoers, then noticed what was happening. She quickly came to Groucho's side, pulled him aside for a brief moment, and then they both returned to the journalist. Groucho then said, "I thought the movie was wonderful."

Audiences want to be on the side of a winner. They don't want to be so unhip as to defend a loser. If you walk onstage and don't sell your punch lines with a strong voice and solid projection, you label yourself an amateur. You give these people the right to reject you. In fact, because of peer pressure, you almost force the audience to turn against you.

They want to go with a "pro," someone who knows what she's doing when she steps behind the microphone.

Sometimes your success or failure can be that delicate. Why take the chance? Project your punch lines. Sell your big laughs.

Now let's study ways for you to learn how to have your jokes heard.

Slow Down.

Most of us speak faster than we think we do. We know what we're going to say and we hear the words in our heads before we ever voice them. The listeners, though, don't. They are hearing your words for the first time, without benefit of knowing what they should be or hearing them formulated in your mind. The listeners depend entirely on your projection and enunciation. If you don't form the words properly, they can't hear them clearly.

This advice to slow down applies to all speakers, not just comedians. When we get nervous—and certainly public speaking makes all of us anxious—we tend to rush our speech.

The first suggestion is to make a conscious effort to speak slowly and distinctly. Speaking more slowly, at a reasonable pace, won't hurt good comedy material. It should enhance it. Jack Benny worked slowly onstage. He had confidence in his material. He wasn't afraid to take his time, to develop a line, because he knew he had a strong payoff. He knew the laugh at the end would justify it. Max Alexander is a newer comedian who works at a delightfully slow pace. He doesn't rush through his set-ups. He works comfortably, and when he gets to his punch lines, they pay off. Because people understand everything he says, they know exactly what he's talking about. His punch lines become that much more effective.

Granted, there are some comics who work frenetically, who deliver their lines quickly. It works for them because they project powerfully and enunciate well. Even though they do rush through their material, they are heard and understood.

It's much better, and safer, to speak more slowly and be understood rather than rush and have the audience not hear important parts of your performance.

There are several reasons why comics tend to rush their delivery.

A good joke wants to be told.

When you have a solid, sure-fire piece of material you want to get it out there. You want the audience to hear it, and applaud, and laugh. You can't wait to hear that explosion of hilarity. Your larynx can't wait. Your tongue can't wait. Your lips can't take time to form the words. You spit the set-up and punch line out there just as fast as humanly possible.

I've noticed this same phenomenon when I play tennis. My opponent will hit a weak shot that anyone could put away for a winner. I flub it. I hit it into the net. Why? How could I miss such an easy shot?

The answer is that I rush. I'm so thrilled at seeing an easy set-up that I speed up. I'm so anxious to hit my winner that I do everything fast and wrong. I take an easy shot and ruin it by rushing.

Comics do the same thing with good jokes. They want to get them out to the audience, so they speak fast. Sometimes it's too fast to be intelligible. When that happens, it hurts the joke. So, it's better to slow down the tempo slightly and have the joke heard—and consequently appreciated.

Comedians tend to over-rehearse, especially with good lines.

You know you've got a powerful gag so you tell it over and over again. You might add a few flourishes. You get confident with it, even cocky. You get so you can tell that gag in your sleep.

You get to know that joke so well that you get slick with it. It trips off your tongue like butter melting over a hot stack of pancakes. Sometimes, though, you get too slick, too fast. The words run together so that the listeners can't appreciate their meaning. The result is that the good joke becomes less effective. When you get so good that you get careless, that's over-rehearsal.

I'll go back to a sports example. You notice that golfers take a long time analyzing and studying putts that are a challenge to them. They'll try to find out which way the grass grain runs and how the greens slope. They'll stand over the putt for sometime before stroking the ball.

Then they get a two-foot putt and rush it. They just walk up and tap the ball, thinking it has to go in and it doesn't. They out-slick themselves.

That's what you might do with jokes that you feel are sure-fire. You rush them. Take a little bit more time with them and *guarantee* that they're sure-fire.

Comics tend to rush when they're bombing.

You try your first few jokes and the crowd is not impressed, so you just want to get this evening over with— as quickly as possible. It's embarrassing up there when the laughs aren't coming. It's painful. You want to end the agony as quickly as you can, so you speak more rapidly. You rush through your routines.

These are the evenings that build character. These are the nights that transform you from an aspiring comic into an experienced pro. The laughs may never come during this set, but that's all right. Your mother surely must have warned you there'd be nights like this. Experiences like this are a challenge. They present an opportunity for you to meet and conquer a worthy foe. This is when you work harder to convert this audience from hostile or indifferent to fans of yours. You may not win, but you don't want to pass up an opportunity to try.

Going back to the sports theme again: Coaches want their teams to play hard, even when they're being blown out of a game. Why? Because it's an opportunity to show their mettle and to practice. To practice for those times when the game will be close, when it will be decided by whichever team has the most stamina, skill, and guts.

And every once in a while a runaway game is pulled out and won by the underdog. Every once in a while, a comedian turns an audience around, pulls laughter from their reluctant bellies.

In any case, a lackluster audience is your chance to practice delivering your material slowly and clearly. Sure, it takes longer, but it's worth it.

Besides, if this is a truly unlikable audience and if your material is really not working, then what better revenge than to make them sit there through it all?

Enunciate.

Some people in comedy believe that any word with a "K" in it is funny. "Chicken" is a funny word. "Hockey puck" is hilarious. If there's any truth to this at all, it might be because words with a "K" are easier to pronounce. You have to bark out a "K." It marks a definite and abrupt end of a syllable, so you are forced to pronounce it.

You can punch out the pronunciation of "chicken." It has a military snap to its enunciation. It's a hard word, a crisp word. "Cornish game hen" is soft. It just kind of dribbles out of your mouth.

Maybe that's why "K" words are funnier.

However, you can't always lean on mechanical words for your comedy. You're going to have to learn to deliver all of your words with crispness and clarity, as if they all had a "K" in them.

After all, these are your punch lines. They're your bread and butter. You want them heard and understood, and you want to deliver them with all the bite that you can give them. You do that by enunciating each word as if it had a "K" in it.

"But," you argue, "how about a comedian like Buddy Hackett?" Hackett certainly doesn't speak with the crispness of a Richard Burton, so how does he get laughs? When's the last time you misunderstood anything that

Buddy Hackett said? He speaks out—slowly. He projects. Perhaps he doesn't speak with proper British precision, but he gives each word its due. In fact, he almost exaggerates each word, each syllable. In his own way, he does enunciate.

One comedy instructor borrowed from the great Greek orator Demosthenes. To overcome a speech impediment, Demosthenes placed pebbles in his mouth and practiced delivering his orations. Each day he'd remove one pebble until he conquered his difficulty. The comedy instructor suggested marbles instead. He said, "Practice your routine with several marbles in your mouth. When you feel improved, remove one marble. When you lose all your marbles, you're a comedian."

I'm not sure you must be that drastic (or that hokey), but you should learn to pronounce your words clearly and distinctly. To be effective, your punch lines must be heard and understood.

Change your jokes, if you must. When I was beginning in comedy, I once wrote a joke that depended on the words "shoulder holster" in the punch line. It was a funny joke. Mercifully, I've forgotten it.

I never could say the words "shoulder" and "holster" together. They came out "sherdel herster" or "shouldal holdal" or some similar gibberish. I came close, but I never got it. Eventually, I dropped the joke.

You may have similar pronunciation blocks. If you do, adjust. Change the punch line, reword it. If your gag absolutely depends on "Frederick Ferdinand Farquart the Fifth fought ferociously to free the frightened, freezing firemen," good luck. If it doesn't, change the payoff to something you can pronounce clearly and cleanly.

Practice Speaking.

I don't mean to practice your comedy routine. Certainly, you should do that, too. But I mean, learn to be eloquent. Most of us aren't.

Sometime, get a tape recorder and turn the sound down on your television while you're watching a sporting event, an ice-skating competition, a dance contest, a fashion show or anything that you're interested in. While you're watching, narrate it. Pretend you're the announcer on this broadcast and you have to be intelligent about your subject and make the event interesting for the listeners.

When you listen to a playback of your recording you'll be amazed at how awkward you sound and at how many times you strained to find the right words. You'll discover that you say dumb things and that you repeat the same words and phrases over and over again.

It's not easy to be an extemporaneous speaker. Of course, stand-up comedy isn't extemporaneous, but the eloquence that you'll gain from this practice will make you a better stage performer.

Once I asked Jay Leno if he had any advice for aspiring performers. His suggestion: "Just try to get stage time. If you want to be a performer, try and get a job as an emcee, or doing commercials, or radio. Just try to get a situation where you can talk. Once you've got a job talking, then try to be funny. It's hard to talk and be funny at the same time . . . your first day."

Here are a few suggestions for learning to speak:

Read aloud.

Hear yourself say the words. Get used to letting your mind and your voice work together. If you're going into a life of performing, you're going to have to get used to cold readings, picking up a script and selling the words with confidence. This is something that to most of us comes only with practice.

As a part of this, I would also suggest that you rehearse aloud. Get used to hearing yourself say the words. It will give your delivery an extra veneer of confidence.

Volunteer for speaking gigs.

- Be a reader in your church.
- Be a public-address announcer at local high-school football games or Little League baseball games.
- Volunteer to read books for the blind.
- Offer to emcee banquets or meetings of any group that you belong to.

Consider joining Toastmasters International or any similar association.

I'm familiar with Toastmasters because I occasionally write articles on humor for their magazine, and I have spoken at several of their local and regional meetings and at their international convention.

Toastmasters is an organization that's open to all. It emphasizes speech skills, both extemporaneous and prepared. I've known several people who were hampered at work because they couldn't deliver a speech in front of any audience, large or small. They were talented and intelligent, but could not make a presentation or chair a meeting.

They joined Toastmasters and in a short while became excellent speakers. The program takes new members through definite steps at their own pace. You can get as much or as little from it as you wish.

Explaining Toastmaster fully would take up too much space in this chapter, but those who want to learn more details can write to:

Toastmasters International
P.O. Box 9052
Mission Viejo, CA 92689-7052

For your jokes to be funny, they must be heard and understood. So, when your jokes don't work, is it because they're not funny or because people aren't hearing them the way you would like them to?

Have a friend monitor your performances—not for comedy, but for clarity. Have that person sit in the audience and listen. Could you be heard? Could you be understood? If not, why not?

When I travel with Bob Hope, we work in some bizarre auditoriums and stadiums. Sometimes, they're open-air theatres. Other times, they're the maintenance deck of an aircraft carrier. They're usually loaded with people.

During the show, I roam around the audience to find out if the sound can be heard distinctly in all areas. If not, we get the sound guys to make some adjustments before the next show or sometimes before the next act.

You have to begin to work on your own sound system—your voice projection and your enunciation. Let the people hear your jokes so you can hear their laughter.

14
HAVE A CONVERSATION
WITH YOUR AUDIENCE

This book is full of advice from a writer standing in the wings to you, the performer, onstage. Here's another bit of advice that has nothing to do with comedy, but is sage counsel nonetheless: Never ask me to sing.

If you do, though, and I sing "Strangers in the Night," I'll probably sing it with hip, finger-snapping phrasing reminiscent of Frank Sinatra. If I sing "Volare," my voice will take on the semi-intoxicated, mellifluous tones of Dean Martin. Should I sing "To All the Girls I've Loved Before," you'll notice a nasal quality to my vocalizing, not unlike Willie Nelson. When I sing "Rocky Mountain High," my voice soars an octave higher. John Denver would be envious. "Forever and Ever Amen" develops a definite country twang in my voice. I may even yodel a bar or two if the spirit moves me. I don't sing "How Am I Supposed to Live Without You"; I wail it like Michael Bolton.

I've got news for me: I'm not Sinatra, Dean Martin, Willie Nelson, John Denver, Randy Travis, or Michael Bolton. And I'm not really singing their songs; I'm mimicking their recordings of those songs. I'm imitating them—badly, naturally, but I'm imitating them.

Earlier, in Chapter 6, we noted how this type of mimicry prevented us from being original. A good vocalist must have an original style. Crosby sounded like Crosby regardless of the song he sang. Whitney Houston does a melody her way—the Whitney Houston way.

Someone once asked Sammy Cahn how to write a Sinatra song. He said you don't. You write a song. When Sinatra sings it, it becomes a Sinatra song.

For a comedian, mimicking another comic or even a current style—like the comedy-club dialect—not only keeps us from being original, it doesn't permit us to be natural. It doesn't allow us to be ourselves, which is what we should be able to do better than anyone else.

Tom Dreesen recommends to comics that they have a conversation with the audience. Speak to them naturally, the way you would to a group of friends. I like this suggestion because it does allow you to be yourself, which by definition gives you originality. It gets you away from formula comedy, where every punch line is delivered with the same inflection, facial expression, and gestures.

By being conversational, you get away from the razzle-dazzle and pyrotechnics some comedians use. You focus on the comedy content of your routine rather than the fringe flamboyancy.

You needn't offend in the other direction, though. You don't have to stand behind the microphone and mimic other conversationalists. You don't have to deliver your lines like Bill Buckley or David Brinkley. You don't have to pretend to be Alistair Cooke. You don't have to sound like a corporate executive at all times. You can be animated, flamboyant, unique and still be conversational.

Phyllis Diller talks to her audience, yet she's zany. Jackie Mason converses with his listeners but with a distinctly unique style. Bill Cosby certainly has an animated style of communication. Dennis Wolfberg punctuates his monologues with almost frightening facial expressions, yet they seem natural. They're unusual, but they are Dennis's way of talking to his audience.

Conversational comedy shouldn't frighten or restrict

you in any way. Talk to the audience any way you want. The key word is *you*. Make it *your* comedic conversational style.

Let's talk a little bit about how you can find and develop your own conversational style.

Listen to Yourself.

You already have a workable conversational style. You use it each time you speak with someone. It's your natural way of thinking and talking, of forming sentences and making gestures and facial expressions. It's probably perfectly fine for your stage presentations, too.

Sometimes we overlook our natural talents in search of something extraordinary. Often the natural talents are more extraordinary than we give them credit for. I've worked with many comedians, several of them legendary stars, and I've found that almost all of them converse exactly the same offstage as on. Their normal speech patterns were good enough to build incredible comedy careers upon them.

This is not to say that you shouldn't or couldn't develop a different stage persona for yourself. It's just a reminder not to cavalierly dismiss the speech style that you already have and have been developing all your life. It has worked for some other pretty successful comics. It just might work for you.

Eliminate Anything That Sounds Like Anyone Else.

Study your act. Study the way you deliver each individual line. When you find anything that sounds like anyone else, change it.

We started this chapter with my singing. If I sing "Volare," I do it like Dean Martin. Even when I try not to, Dean Martin's style sneaks in. You may face the same problem. You may study a line, notice that you're delivering that punch line in the traditional way, try to change it, and get frustrated. You'll swear there's no other way to deliver that line properly. Work on it because there is another way. You just haven't found it yet.

Remember Sammy Cahn's words: When Sinatra sings that song, it becomes a Sinatra song." When you do a line, it should become *your* line.

Find a different inflection and tone for each of your punch lines. Try saying them different ways. Deliver the line naturally, the way you would if you were just sitting and talking to an acquaintance instead of an audience.

When you eliminate everything that sounds like someone else, you're left with your own individual style.

Of course, you don't have to change every single line. If you can, fine. You'll be truly unique. But if you can't, you'll still change enough of your routine to give it a conversational tone. Some of your lines may be reminiscent of the comedy-club dialect, but overall, your act will have its own conversational mark.

You needn't be afraid of changing. It won't destroy the humor.

Let's go back to my singing again. "Volare" should sound like Dean Martin. It must have that devil-may-care lilt to the voice. That's what we may think, but it's not necessarily so. "Volare" is a finely crafted song regardless of who sings it. The melody is there; the harmony is there. It has a worth of it's own apart from Martin's phrasing.

So do your jokes. They have merit. They have comedic content. They don't have to be delivered as Rodney Dangerfield would say them . . . or Jerry Seinfeld . . . or Richard Lewis. If they're well-constructed gags, they'll sound good the way you say them, too.

In golf, each club is designed for a specific purpose. If you swing smoothly, rhythmically, and correctly, the

club will do what it's supposed to do. It will lift the ball
so high, and drive it so far. However, if you try to lift the
ball higher than the club allows or hit it farther than the
club permits, you destroy your basic swing and hit the ball
improperly.

This can sometimes happen with comics. They have
a basically sound joke, a joke that will get a certain response from an audience. The comic tries to augment that
laugh with unnecessary gimmickry, and it destroys the balance. It hurts rather than helps the gag.

This doesn't mean that you can't help a joke with a
facial expression, a gesture, or a unique reading. Certainly
a good golfer can do things with the club that we weekend hackers can't. But it does mean that a joke has a value
of its own. Delivering that joke with your conversational
style—rather than someone else's—will not diminish that
gag's inherent value.

Many beginning golfers are amazed when they discover that when they swing through the ball with a relaxed, easy tempo, the ball flies truer and longer. They
don't have to overpower it or muscle it to get added distance. So comics are surprised that when they "throw
away" a line—deliver it in a relaxed, easy conversational
tone—it delivers more punch.

I also have a theory—admittedly, untried and
unsubstantiated—that those comedians who last the longest are those you would enjoy having over to the house
for dinner.

These are the ones you could sit down with over a
cup of coffee and dessert and enjoy a conversation with.
They'd be intelligent and occasionally get off a zinger or
two that would keep the dialogue lighthearted.

There are some others who are delightfully funny, yet
who would drive you and the family bonkers before you
got past the soup and salad. You'd either throw them out
before the entrée was served or have the dinner end in
a fight.

I don't have to supply the names. You can apply this litmus test yourself. You can predict which comedy notables you think will last and which won't.

Some comedy devices are so unnatural that, even though they're amusing, they're wearying. Audiences tire of them quickly. These comedy stars can burn brightly and then burn out.

If you want to make it and stay awhile in the business, you might consider a more conversational comedy style—one where you might be invited to my place for dinner.

15
TAKE CHARGE OF YOUR
AUDIENCE

When I was a kid, I thought all a musical conductor had
to do was wave his wand and try to muss his hair in
tempo. Bandleaders were a joke, I thought. They tapped
their foot, wiggled the baton, and smiled at the audience.
It was easy.

I still don't know much about music, but I've learned
that conducting is more than just show. The person fac-
ing the orchestra is definitely in charge. That person controls the performance. Not just the melody and the tempo,
but the feel of the piece, the mood of the selection, the
emotion of the music.

To do this effectively, the conductor must know the
overall composition. The person on the podium has to
understand what the composer is trying to convey and
how. The conductor has to understand the message of the
music and how to get that across to the listeners. He or
she must know the melody, the harmony, and the soul of
the composition.

The conductor also must know the instrumentation.
When do the violins come in? The horns? The drums?
Which should dominate the harmony? Which should sneak
into the composition and which should blare into it with
gusto? He or she must be familiar with the strengths and
limitations of each instrument in the orchestra.

The conductor, too, should know the orchestra, the

people who sit in the chairs and play the instruments. How do they play? What do they play best? Certainly most professional symphony orchestras have qualified musicians who should be able to handle any composition, but how about high-school orchestras? A conductor would get better results selecting easier pieces that he knows they can play well, rather than impossible selections that might embarrass them.

When a comedian takes center stage, he or she is conducting the audience. Just as the conductor is exhorting the musicians to deliver music that blends into an exciting musical unit, so you are urging your listeners to laugh at the right places, applaud on demand, and deliver whatever responses you feel are required to deliver an exciting entertainment package.

When I worked on one specific variety show, we did what we used to call "slice of life" sketches. These were pieces that were filled with emotion instead of laughs. They were pieces that delivered a message instead of hilarity. I hated them.

I always felt they were an admission that the writing staff couldn't come up with sufficient funny lines to write a sketch, so we came up with a message. Nevertheless, the producer included them in the show.

I watched from the control booth once as the cast performed one of these "slice of life" pieces. The audience sat quietly. There was nothing to laugh at. When the sketch ended, they continued to sit quietly.

The producer was excited in the booth. He said, "The audience loved it." I said, "How do you know?"

They didn't do anything; they just sat there. Oh, naturally, they applauded when the "applause" sign was flashed above their heads, but they did that after unfunny sketches, too.

I was prejudiced. I was a comedy writer and felt that comedy sketches were better than "meaningful," artsy one-act plays. But now I must reluctantly admit that this producer had a point. Silence is a valid audience reaction.

As a comedian, you usually want laughter. You certainly appreciate applause. You might even be thrilled with some hooting, hollering, foot stomping, arm waving, and barking like we see on "The Arsenio Hall Show." However, there will be times when you want silence. There will be occasions when you'll want a smile rather than a raucous laugh. Sometimes you'll be thrilled to see some of the audience choke up and perhaps a tear overflow from someone's eyes. There are all sorts of subtle reactions that you may want from your listeners.

The point is that you—the person behind the microphone—will have to extract these reactions from your audience. You are in charge. You will have to orchestrate these responses.

Like the conductor, to do this effectively, you must know your own act, not just memorize it and know which chunk follows which chunk, and which joke comes next. You must understand your act. Know its pacing. Understand when you should go slowly, when you should build, and when you should deliver a punch line like the crack of a whip.

Let's talk about each aspect separately.

Know Your Overall Act.

When you work as a comedian, you want the audience to appreciate you when your act is over. That's why a standing ovation after a performance is such a tribute. It shows that the audience listened and watched everything you did and they enjoyed it. Their standing applause tells you that they appreciated your evening of entertainment.

If they enjoyed your opening joke, and then your fifth joke, and the routine about going to a near-sighted dentist, and then the third joke from the end, but felt cheated and disappointed when you said, "Thank you and good night," you feel no satisfaction for that.

Conversely, if they sat in silence for two or three minutes of your act, but roared when you reached the punch line, that's good. If they were confused for a while, but then laughed and applauded when you justified your story, that's great. If, when you were done with your set, they were glad they saw it, you're a smash.

Sure, the whole is the sum of its parts, but there's no axiom that says that all those parts must be equal. One network executive said to me after the debut of a variety show that I produced with my partner, "You know what was wrong with this show? Some parts of it were funnier than others."

I said, "Really? We tried to give all parts of it exactly the same funniness."

Sure, some parts are funnier than others. You take a terrible movie and think back and you'll admit that some parts were funnier than others. You can do the same, though, with a hit comedy movie. There are ups and downs in any comedy presentation. Johnny Carson used to refer to them with tongue in cheek as the hills and valleys of comedy. They do exist. They have to. If all parts were equally funny, the presentation would be monotonous.

The secret, though, is to make sure that the end result, the overall effect, is pleasant, is entertaining, is funny. To do that, you have to be familiar with the overall act.

Tommy Armour, the renowned golf instructor, tells a story in one of his books about a student of his. This gentleman was a businessman with a passion for golf, and he hit the ball well. Tommy Armour says of him that he was a good hitter but a bad player.

One day, in a fit of golfer's bravado, this gentleman proclaimed that he could play a round of golf that day and come in under ninety. Naturally, as happens in golf clubhouses, some wagers were made. Armour placed a sizable bet supporting his pupil. One of the conditions of play was that, since Tommy Armour had bet a large amount, he would be allowed to play the round with the braggart and coach him.

The student got off a long drive on the first tee, but

slightly in the rough on the right side of the fairway. He pulled out a five-iron to try to reach the green in two shots and possibly sink the putt for a birdie, or one under par. It wouldn't be a bad start.

However, his coach, Tommy Armour, said, "Put that club away."

The student argued: "I've got a shot at a birdie."

Armour said, "You've got a much bigger chance of missing the shot. Then you'll have another tough shot to make just to get on the green." He advised him to hit an easier shot out into the fairway in front of the green, then he'd have a much easier shot onto the green and possibly one-putt for a par.

The student played that way and parred the hole.

At each hole after that, the teacher would have to argue with the student, but he won out and the gentleman finished the round at seventy-nine, quite a bit under ninety.

If you don't know golf, you may not appreciate some of the details of that story, but you should understand this: The student was approaching the game shot-by-shot. The teacher was admonishing him to look at the overall round of golf. The teacher was advising him to do whatever was required to guarantee a low score. Golf doesn't reward players for occasional great shots; it rewards those who play well all day and score well.

Likewise, an audience doesn't reward a comic who scores with an occasional great joke; it rewards those who entertain them while they're onstage. There's a big difference. This golfer discovered it when he saw his final score for eighteen holes. You'll see it when you leave the stage.

How do you know your overall act? Well, you rehearse it. You know what you're trying to deliver at each moment of the act. Sometimes you're getting laughs, at other times you may only be setting up laughs. Both are important. At times you may be going for pathos. Sometimes a hint of a tear makes the laughter that much more powerful.

There can be many different colorations to your act; you should know and be aware of them.

Then, too, you learn about your overall performance by studying the audience. How do they react? Are they waiting for your punch lines or are you losing them? If you're not keeping their interest, you must find out why. Perhaps you're going too long without laughs. Then change the structure of your act or add some laughs to the piece you're doing.

Listen to the audience and learn how you have to adjust the pacing of your act.

Know Your Jokes.

This may sound like an admonition that is so basic that it is unnecessary. Believe me, it isn't. Many times I've had performers ask me, after delivering a line hundreds of times at rehearsals and onstage, what was so funny about a particular punch line. When I'd explain the meaning of the joke, they'd say, "Really? I didn't know that."

The strange part, to me: If they didn't know what the punch line meant, why were they telling this joke?

At least you have to know the punch line of your joke. Again, that may seem obvious, but it often isn't. The punch line dictates your set-up line. Some performers, though, will ad-lib the set-up or change it to something close. They have no idea that, in so doing, they're destroying the comedy.

There was an example of that on the old "Ed Sullivan Show." Singer Jack Jones guested on the show. Jack's father, Alan, was also a well-known singer years before.

For a light comedy touch, after Jack Jones completed his number, he crossed over to shake hands with Ed Sullivan. Sullivan was then supposed to ask, "Wasn't Alan Jones your father?" Jack was to respond, "He still is."

When Jack Jones did cross to Sullivan, the host asked him, "*Isn't* Alan Jones your father?" All Jack could answer was, "Yes."

By not knowing, or understanding, the punch line, Ed Sullivan blew the set-up and consequently destroyed the joke.

The punch line is your whole reason for beginning any story or joke in the first place. Everything you say and do should lead to that payoff. To do that properly, you must know what the punch line is.

More than that, though, you should understand the comedy and the mechanics of the joke. You should know why it is funny and how to say it in its funniest way.

This doesn't mean that you have to be able to explain in intricate, painstaking detail the humor of the gag. That's almost impossible. I know. I've written what I've considered to be some pretty funny one-liners and then the comic would ask, "What's funny about this line?" It's an unanswerable question. Once you're asked that, the funniness drains out of the joke.

Nevertheless, you should have at least a general appreciation for the humor in your joke. Only when you have that understanding of the gag can you present it confidently and correctly.

Realizing the mechanics of the gag can help you deliver it more effectively, also. It helps you in phrasing the line properly, using the appropriate gestures, and emphasizing the right words.

Let me give you one example of this. In my talk I tell a story about a man who loses his temper and says something terrible to his wife. He says, in a fit of anger, "I don't understand how someone like you can be so incredibly beautiful and at the same time so incredibly stupid."

When I deliver that line, the audience gasps.

The payoff: "My wife says, 'I think God made me incredibly beautiful so you'd be attracted to me. And I think he made me incredibly stupid so I'd be attracted to you."

It gets a big audience response because it relieves the tension created by the set-up line. It gets an especially large reaction from the women because it champions their cause.

The tendency is to deliver this line with the emphasis on the words "me" and "you." That's the basic comparison of the joke—here's why you're attracted to *me*; here's why I'm attracted to *you.*

The traditional comedy reading of that line would be to emphasize that difference and punch those two words in the delivery.

However, I felt the people in the audience would recognize that. Once I said, "God made me beautiful so you'd be attracted to *me*," accenting the word "me," the joke would be over. The audience would recognize the comparison, anticipate, and immediately know that the punch line would be, "And he made me so stupid so I'd be attracted to *you*," stressing the word "you." They'd get ahead of the joke, ruin the surprise element, and change the reaction from a big laugh to some groans, chuckles, whispers, and a few weak laughs.

So, I cheat. I accent the word "attracted." It not only hides the punch line, it sets up a different anticipation in the audience's minds. Then when I do hit the payoff, it's a surprise to the audience. It gets a much bigger response.

You're presenting your lines primarily for an audience reaction. Therefore, it's wise to learn as much as you can about each joke. Know the mechanics of it and study how to deliver it most effectively. It pays off in laughs.

Know Your Audience.

You've probably heard the story about the mother who heard terrible yelping coming from the puppy in another room. When she rushed in to find out what the matter was, she saw her young son pulling on the poor creature's tail.

She yelled, "Junior, stop pulling the puppy's tail."

The boy answered, "I'm just holding on, Mom. The puppy's doing all the pulling."

Your audience has got to do some of the pulling, too.

You are the conductor and you have to put them all to work. You must get them laughing. You have to tell them when to laugh. While you're onstage, they are your responsibility.

You should get to know them. I don't mean you should introduce yourself to each one of them as they come in the door and ask a few questions about each of them. No. But you can get to know an audience in general.

For instance, if you're playing The Laff Stop outside of Houston, Texas, you can find out what sort of crowd goes there. Are they young? What income range do they fit into? What sort of work do most of them do? Are they mostly married or dating? What kind of music do they dig? What movies would they like? What celebrities would they know?

Certainly you can appreciate that they would be different in many ways from a show that you might do for a banquet room full of insurance-company executives.

They, in turn, would be unlike the audience you would face if you're doing a show for the local retirement home.

If you're the conductor of this orchestra of laughers, it's up to you to learn as much as you can about them.

Once you do your research, you still have to get these people to do their work. You must get them to listen to you onstage, to pay attention. You do that by getting their attention. We've already talked about how to do that in this book. This will be just a brief reminder. You get their attention first of all by being heard. You speak up and project. You speak clearly so that they can understand what you're saying. You get their attention with a powerful opening. Remember?

Next you have to merit their respect. You must convince them that you, the person behind the microphone, are in charge. Again, we've covered this before. You do this by being confident onstage, well-rehearsed. You present an aura of authority. And you also show that you care about this particular audience.

Next you must give them direction, you must tell them when to laugh. That means that you know where the jokes are and you deliver them so that the audience, too, knows where they are.

Once you do that, you must challenge them to laugh. Sometimes it takes a little doing, but you're the person in charge. You have to let the listeners know that you just told a funny joke. You not only think it's funny, you *know* it's funny. If they're not laughing, something is wrong with them.

You must make your audience do their work. When I first got into television, many of my gags were edited out. When I asked the producer about this, he said that they were "think" jokes. His conclusion was that if people had to think, they wouldn't laugh. They wouldn't want to take the time to think the jokes through.

I say, those are your best jokes. Those are the ones that force your audience to do its work. However, you're in charge. You must get them to do their work. You must force them to think—and to laugh.

16
WHAT TO DO WHEN THE
JOKES DON'T WORK

It's time now for a chilling, brutal dose of comedy reality. You can study this book from cover to cover, adopt all of its precepts, commit it to memory if you like. You can study under the most knowledgeable and capable of comedy teachers. You can write, edit, and polish a dynamite routine. Practice, rehearse, and refine it to flawless perfection. You can develop your timing until it's impeccable. Still, you will have nights when the jokes don't work. It just happens.

One time I was speaking with Bob Hope about a young comic who was a potential candidate to guest on one of the Hope specials. Hope said, "Do you know him?"

I said, "Yes, I've seen him several times."

"What do you think?"

I said, "Well, he has some brilliant material, some great routines. Yet, I've seen him some nights when he was just Okay."

Hope was silent for a beat or two on the other end of the phone, then he said, "Gene, that's all of us."

He's right. It happens, and it happens to all comics. I lectured one time to a woman's group. ("Lecture" is a pompous word for the formalized talk that I give. Actually, it amounts to a stand-up routine about the shows and people I've written comedy for.) The talk was in a movie theatre. The aisles fanned out so that the front-row center section consisted of only about nine seats.

As I lectured, I tried to cover the entire auditorium, working left and right and playing to the people in the back row. I discovered, though, that in trying to project, I was neglecting those people up front. So at one point, I looked down to talk directly to the nine people in that front row.

All of them had their heads back, mouths open, and were sound asleep.

Another cruel fact of comedy life—an offshoot of this one, actually—is that it's always painful when this happens. We were once preparing to tape a Bob Hope special from a remote location, and we were rehearsing the entire show with a live audience. We felt this would give us a better idea of where to make cuts and changes to sharpen the actual show.

The rehearsal audience was much different from the audience that we expected for the show. They were mostly youngsters who had come in to see the musical acts. The evening audience would be a sophisticated, black-tie crowd. Consequently, the monologue played a little soft.

Between acts, Bob Hope complained that the lines weren't working. I tried to reassure him that the jokes were written for the invited audience, not this rehearsal crowd. I said, "I'm sure the jokes will play well at the regular show." Hope said, "I don't care about the regular show. I'm suffering out there now."

Often there are reasons why the audience is apathetic—reasons beyond your control. It could be a bad sound system, bad lighting, troublemakers in the audience, people who don't speak English (that actually happened to a client and me when I was writing nightclub material).

However, it doesn't pay to dismiss a bad show too quickly as someone else's fault. You get no educational benefit from cavalierly dismissing this as the room's problem or the audience's. Blame yourself first.

Even with a substandard sound system, could you have gotten this crowd? How could you have overcome bad lighting? Was there something you could have said or done to quiet a rowdy table that was distracting the rest of the audience?

Not all of your performances will have ideal conditions, so it pays you to learn how to entertain under less-than-perfect circumstances. That's how you gain experience. That's how you learn to be a pro.

Even more basic: Were your jokes funny enough? Was your delivery sharp? It's very tempting to blame the room or the crowd for our poor performances.

Regardless of the reason—whether it's yours, the club's, or the crowd's—these painful sessions will happen. What do you do and what don't you do when the jokes don't work?

Take It Like a Pro.

Bombing is painful. It always was and it always will be.

It's also distressing to hear your dentist say, "You have a cavity." What do you do, though? You make an appointment, take your shot of Novocaine, open wide, and put up with that irritating grinding and scraping.

You really have no choice. The cavity exists and it needs this sort of repair work.

Onstage, you have no choice either. This is one of those nights that you knew would happen sometime. Other comics warned you about it. Now it's here.

You take your medicine like a good little comedy soldier. You endure the anguish for this one set, knowing that it builds character. It should make you a better comic. It should help turn you into a pro.

Have Some Fun with It.

Basically, audiences are good people. They're pulling for you. One reason is that they paid to get in to see you. If you're a smash, that means their money was well spent. Also, they want to have some fun. You're the person who is supposed to provide that fun. So they want you to be good.

Mostly, though, they're good folks who appreciate how tough it is to stand onstage and get laughs. They're sympathetic and they're pulling for you.

Therefore, they know how painful a few bombs can be. They understand and are forgiving, provided that you understand and are forgiving, too.

If you accept the reality of the situation and go along with it, they'll be on your side.

Some people suspected that Johnny Carson used to intentionally add some clunkers to his opening monologues on "The Tonight Show" just so he could play with it. He'd kid himself, go into his dance, and many people laughed harder at that than at his one-liners. They enjoyed it.

I don't think Carson told bad jokes on purpose, but I do believe that when some of the jokes didn't deliver, he turned it to an advantage rather than a disaster.

It might benefit you to have a few standard cover lines for when a joke fails. I've seen Bob Hope do a few during his television monologues. A joke will get noticeably less response than he expected, and he'll glare at the audience and say, "You'll never hear that joke again. *Nobody* will ever hear that joke again." Then he'll tell the cue-card guy to "throw that card away."

The audience is not only forgiving, but they love being on the inside. They're thrilled to be there to see a Bob Hope joke get kidded like that.

Don't Whine.

There's a member of our tennis club who is a mediocre player—like most of us—but he's dreadful to play with.

Few of the members want to play with him, not because he makes bad shots—we all do that—but because when he does, he whines like a child who can't have what he wants.

After he hits the ball into the net, he moans and wails and practically sobs. It's annoying, disconcerting and takes the fun out of the game for the other players in the foursome.

Whining, griping, complaining turn people off. Do it onstage and you'll turn your audience off. If you're bombing, you have enough trouble onstage already. Don't make it worse.

Of course, misery loves company, so if you're having a miserable night, you want to make the listeners suffer, too. Don't. Suffer silently and alone.

Don't Let It Throw You.

I attended a speaker's showcase a few years ago and watched many professional speakers offer samples of their talks. A showcase is where buyers are invited to attend and listen to several speakers present their talks or excerpts from their talks. Presumably, this will entice these people to hire some of these speakers for upcoming conventions, seminars, workshops, or whatever.

For the speaker, of course, it's an important gig because it can lead to sales. They can book many speeches from a single showcase.

One friend of mine stood to deliver a half-hour sample of his talents to the assembled buyers. About three minutes into his presentation, his microphone broke. It fell off the stand and shattered on the floor.

The sponsors of the event quickly replaced it with another mike that worked perfectly. However, the speaker didn't. He was so shaken by the incident that he lost total concentration. For the next twenty-seven minutes of his talk, he was tentative, he faltered, he fumbled, and phumphered. He was terrible.

Why? His speech was interrupted for only a few seconds. The audience was understanding. They ran seminars and conferences; they knew how equipment can be uncooperative. They were sympathetic.

Besides, this tiny gaffe provided the speaker with an opportunity for humor. It could have allowed him to show these buyers his poise, how he could be cool under fire. Instead he collapsed.

Don't Give Up.

There's probably no worse feeling in entertainment than to be onstage telling jokes and getting no laughs. The silence is gut-wrenching. But wait . . . there is a worse feeling. That is to have a table of friends or relatives in the audience who feel obliged to laugh. The resulting "mercy" laugh is worse than no response at all.

But there's a well-respected show-business maxim that says, "The show must go on." That doesn't mean only that the curtain must go up and the performers must be onstage. It means that the "show," the performance, must go on. It's advising everyone: If you're onstage, you must perform. You owe it to the audience to give them your best.

If they don't appreciate your efforts, that's their concern. You, though, should deliver with all the gusto you have. That's your concern. That's your responsibility.

Hanging in there is for your benefit, too. Phyllis Diller once told me, "There's no such thing as a good beginning comic. They're all terrible." This is not a condemnation of young comics; it's a statement of fact. Phyllis was once a beginning comic, and she admits that she was terrible and had a lot to learn. But you become a good comic through experience. These painful evenings help you grow into a good comedian. They help you develop showmanship. But not if you give up.

Don't Blame the Audience.

It's not their fault that you're stinking the room up.

I listened to many comedians in a comedy club one evening, and one young lady got angry at the crowd because her set wasn't going over as well as she would have liked. She told us about it, too. She told us about it after each joke that didn't work.

After one joke that got only a mediocre reaction at best, she said, "Oh, my God, that's a funny joke. What the hell is wrong with you people?" After another a few lines later, she said, "I give up. You people are a waste of time." She continued on through her set with similar comments.

It should have occurred to her that these same people she was chastising laughed at the comics who were on before her. We wanted to have a good time there that night. We paid to listen to some funny comics. We laughed at others, so we knew what sounded funny to us.

That's probably what bothered her—that she wasn't as well received as the others on the bill. So, she took it out on us.

In so doing, she sealed her own unpleasant fate. First, her comments created tension in the room. They killed any atmosphere for laughter that did exist. People were uneasy after her tirades. They weren't relaxed enough to laugh at her.

Second, she made herself the enemy. Some of us were probably rooting for her. We wanted her to pull out of this comedy quagmire she was in and score with a few good one-liners. Once she attacked, though, she alienated any and all supporters.

In business, the rule of thumb is that the customer is always right. In comedy, the audience is. Don't try to convince them otherwise.

Don't Blame the Writers.

Admittedly, I'm prejudiced. I usually stand with the writers and am offended by those who rely on them and then attack them. However, that's not why I'm advising you, the comic, to lay off them.

Earlier we said that you should appear onstage as the take-charge person. People in the audience respect that. They appreciate your authority.

And you should be in charge. That means that you take full responsibility for whatever you say and do onstage. You tell a joke because you want to tell a joke, because you believe in that joke, because you think it's funny. Not because some writer forced you to tell it.

To blame the writers robs you of some of the command you should have while at the microphone. You can't pretend to be the leader and then hide behind the writers at the first sign of trouble.

We were rehearsing a Bob Hope special in Hollywood when one of the jokes in a sketch got groans from the crew. At a break, Hope came to the foot of the stage, looked down at all the writers huddled together in the audience, and asked for a rewrite of the offensive line. Then he said, "Who wrote that line?"

None of us confessed.

Hope persisted. "Come on," he said, "I just want to know who wrote that terrible line?"

I looked up at Hope and said, "I just want to know who picked it."

Hope flashed his trademark sneer at me and said, "You're right, you know, and I'll get you for it."

Besides, picking on your writers, unless it's done in an obvious spirit of fun, is an act of comedy cowardice that the audience picks up on. It chips away at your credibility.

At a variety-show rehearsal, a well-known comic was doing a piece that our writing staff prepared for him. It was playing beautifully, then he ad-libbed. That line got nothing. He immediately turned to the star of the show and said, "That's the one line your writers gave me and it bombs."

Have some class. Don't blame the writers.

Work Harder.

I recently heard some radio excerpts of Al Jolson, who arguably was the greatest showman of his time. I've heard of him, as you probably have, but I never really knew his act. Yet, as I listened to those tapes, one thing became apparent—when the man sang a song, he sold a song. When he spoke, and especially when he sang, there was excitement. Whether he was a great vocalist or not, I don't know, but he made something happen. He worked at his craft and he worked hard. He was going to entertain you whether you wanted to be entertained or not.

I saw the same thing happen once when I was working on "The Carol Burnett Show." Sammy Davis was our guest star one week, and he enjoyed doing the show. On Wednesday, after rehearsal, he called for all of us on the show to go to Stage 31 at CBS. None of us wanted another meeting. It was the end of the day and we were anxious to start home.

When we got to Stage 31, we saw that a bandstand was prepared and several musicians entered and began warming up. Then Sammy came center stage and said, "I've enjoyed working with you people so much, I'm going to pay you back the best way I know how." With that he began his nightclub act.

Quietly we all moaned. We were tired from working on the show. We didn't want to stay for Sammy's act. He could just send each of us a box of chocolates or something.

Then he went to work. He gave us an hour of electrifying entertainment. He made us enjoy the show.

That's why you have to keep working hard even on the nights when nothing seems to be working. Because that's how you learn to create magic. That's how you become one of those great showmen who can entertain an audience that doesn't want to be entertained.

Part Four

And You . . .

17
LEARN FROM OTHERS

When I was a kid playing grade-school basketball, I fancied myself a pretty good ballplayer. I don't know if my colleagues fancied me that good or not, but it didn't matter. My ego was big enough to support my own fantasy.

I used to play regularly against another youngster who was about my size and my weight, except he was a much better ballplayer. He was quick, clever, and a big scorer. I hated him.

Whenever we played against each other, he humiliated me. So what else could I do? I'd take a swing at him.

Finally, my coach had had enough. He had a talk with me. He said, "That kid's a pretty good ballplayer, isn't he?"

I had to admit that he was.

The coach said, "Instead of starting a fight with him, why don't you watch him? Learn from him?"

What a great idea, I thought. This guy is pretty smart for a coach. Why didn't I think of that.

When I was envious and angry, I learned nothing. When I studied my opponent, though, I added a few of his maneuvers to my own bag of basketball tricks. By learning from him I became a better player.

The same can happen with aspiring comics.

I've worked with a few beginning comics, and I've visited comedy clubs with them to watch their performances. Occasionally, at these shows I'll see a standout performance. One comedian will be the favorite of the show. The audience loves everything this person does at the mike.

After the show, I'll discuss the performance of my comics, offering comments and suggestions. Then I'll talk about the show this standout comic did. My comics will get angry and refuse to talk about this colleague's performance. They'll accuse the other person of chicanery. "They like those jokes because they're dirty." "That comic kisses up to the audience." "That comedian kisses up to the club owner." "That comic steals material." They'll accuse this particular comic of everything except being a "basket hanger." They'd do that, too, if they knew what it meant.

They're upset because this performer is showing them up onstage, just as my opponent showed me up in the gymnasium. They're envious, they're hurt, they're angry, and they're frustrated. They're disappointed with themselves because they're unable to do what this comic is doing.

In reality, this performer is not showing them up. A stand-up comedian's job is to entertain each audience as well as he or she possibly can. That's all this comic is doing. In fact, he's showing them how to entertain, how to get audience reaction, how to get solid laughs.

My basketball foe was showing me how to play the game, too. But so long as I was envious, I learned nothing. In fact, he exploited my anger and frustration. He used it against me. The more I fumed, the easier it was for him to take advantage of me and score. Once I learned to learn from him, I evened out the contest somewhat.

You have to bury your ego, control your envy, check your anger, and *learn.*

What do people like about this comic's performance? Is it the personality? Is it energy? What? How do you find out?

Ask the audience.

Ask the people who watched and enjoyed the performance. I was certainly willing to talk about what I had
seen and appreciated. I even initiated the conversation.
My comedian friends, though, shut off the conversation.
If you do, you're missing a great chance to learn.

Discuss outstanding comedy performances with listeners. Find out what people appreciate and applaud. This
may help you discover bits and chunks that might help
your act.

Ask the comic.

I guarantee that if you catch a performer immediately
after a well-received show, he or she will be more than
willing to talk about it. Get them started and you may never
shut them up, in fact. Find out why this comic does what
he or she does. If there's a signature bit in the act, learn
how it came about. What prompted it? Has it changed since
the comic first introduced it? Research with that person the
history of the act and the various routines in it.

I worked with one comedian who interrupted the taping of a show to ask the audience if they would like to
stay to be part of a routine that he was going to tape to
send to a birthday party for the governor of the state. He
said, "I can't be at the party, but I'm taping this little comedy bit and they'll show it at the banquet."

The audience was thrilled and, of course, they stayed
and enjoyed the routine. I said to the comic after the show,
"I didn't know we were doing a bit for the governor."

He said, "We aren't."

I said, "Then what was that announcement all about?"

He said, "The audience was getting tired and I wanted
them up and bright for this routine, so I told them about
this."

He noticed that they were wearying because the taping session ran long. By concocting a white lie, he revi-

talized them by making them part of a piece of material that would be played for the governor. The audience felt they were on the "inside," and they responded with enthusiastic applause and laughter when we needed it.

It was a gimmick, indeed. However, it was a gimmick that I never knew about before. I learned by asking the comic.

Analyze the successful comedian's choice of topics.

That might be what the audience appreciates. I once worked with a writer who was a "fallen away" comedian. He once complained to me about a comic who scored better than he did at a nightclub. He said, "I was doing a smart, sophisticated routine that featured a humorous exchange between William Shakespeare and Voltaire. This other clown was doing a stupid routine about leaving for work and accidentally picking up a bag of garbage instead of his lunch bag. Yet the audience is laughing like hell at this guy's piece of garbage. And I couldn't figure out why."

What I couldn't figure out was why a comedian would go into a nightclub and do a routine about Shakespeare and Voltaire. I'm not sure these two people enter into the everyday conversations of comedy-club patrons. Maybe, just maybe, the bag of garbage was closer to what they wanted to laugh about.

I know that artists proclaim that they paint what they want to paint. Writers boast that they write for themselves. I'm not sure I believe them 100 percent. There's something to be said for being true to yourself in any project, but there are some rewards in having it accepted by the people, too. In comedy, especially, you can work for your own gratification if you like, but it can seem awfully unfunny when you're the only one in the room laughing. You have to please the audience.

If you listen to those who are pleasing the crowd, you may discover what that crowd enjoys hearing. Set parameters for yourself—perhaps somewhere between

Shakespeare and a sack of suet—and then work for yourself, but within those parameters.

Suppose, though, that you do study and analyze your more-successful colleagues and discover that you don't want to do what they've done to achieve success. You may not agree with their methods. You may not permit yourself to do the kind of material that they and their audiences seem to relish. What then?

Thomas Edison was reported to have tried some 5,000 different types of filaments that didn't work when he was trying to perfect the light bulb. A reporter asked him if he was discouraged. He said, "No. I've discovered 5,000 things that won't work."

You're learning more about yourself and your own act even when you're discovering things that you don't want to do. You're defining parameters for what you do want to do in comedy. You're still searching, as Edison was, but you've found things that don't work. That frees you to focus your search for humor that does work for you, your style, and your audience.

Suppose, too, that you analyze a successful comedy cohort and discover that he or she is gaining fame because he or she is just funnier and more talented than you are. You can still learn from that person. You can still become a better comic by attentively listening to that comedian.

Suppose, for example, that Jack Nicklaus offered to give you a few hours of golf lessons. Maybe Chris Evert would volunteer some of her time to teach you the game of tennis. Would you refuse? Would you say, "I'll never be the golfer that Nicklaus is or the tennis pro that Evert is, therefore, I can learn nothing from them"? Certainly you wouldn't. You'd have to admit that Jack and Chris are better athletes in their respective sports than you'll ever be, but they can still help you to improve the quality of your game. They can make you a better competitor.

My school-days basketball opponent was much more

accomplished than I was, yet the lessons he taught me improved my playing—not to his level, but a step above my former level. That's progress. It's a definite plus.

And this phenomenon works conversely, also. When Magic Johnson played basketball in the NBA, he was considered among its greatest stars. He was certainly better than most of those he played against. Now that he's a commentator on the NBA games, I notice that he knows all the tricks and moves of those he played against. Why? Because he studied them. Even though he was a better all-around player than they were, he could still learn some maneuvers, some strategies.

You can learn from all of your colleagues, good and bad. Every comic who steps onstage does some things well and other things not so well. You can learn from all of them.

I notice, too, in working with some of today's comics, a resentment for the comedians of the past. They're old-fashioned, passé. The newer comics seemed determined to prove that "We're funnier, we're more inventive, we're making more of a social statement than the fuddy-duddies of yesterday." They may be right. Time usually brings improvement because we adopt the skills of those who went before and add to them. Nevertheless, we can all still learn from the legends of a few years ago.

The older comics have something to offer today's comics. They were good. They had to be outstanding to achieve the success they enjoyed. Show business has always been competitive. It was in vaudeville days; it is today. Stardom was not something that you were appointed to in the old days; it was something you fought for and achieved through hard work. These people knew what they were doing and they did it well. Today's comics can learn much about today by studying the stars of yesterday.

One thing the older comedians can boast of that

today's stars can't is longevity. No matter how successful a young comedian is right now, there is no guarantee that he or she will be around or even remembered ten years from now. Some comics have been powerful for brief periods and then disappeared. It can happen to anyone at anytime. The older comics have lasted. That can't be denied. It should be respected.

Experience is a great teacher, but it doesn't always have to be your experience. You can learn from others, too. You can learn from the good and the bad; the old and the new; the ones you like and the ones you dislike. Today's comics and yesterday's comics, if you study them well, can help you become tomorrow's comic.

18
LEARN FROM EACH PERFORMANCE

The football coach at our local high school was celebrating his twenty-fifth wedding anniversary. He and his wife had just returned from a second honeymoon trip to Hawaii and the school held a banquet in their honor. One of the high-school football players was the emcee and he opened the festivities by saying, "The Coach and his wife have just returned from a second honeymoon in Hawaii. We're not sure whether they had a good time or not. The Coach wants to wait until he reviews the films."

That kid deserves credit for creating a clever, funny, entertaining line. That's the kind of solid opening line that we talked about in Chapter 12. It applies to this event, this person, this audience.

This line also contains a lesson for all of us, though. It reminds us that most organized teams, from high school to professional, do review game films. Play by play they study past performances. They review which plays worked, which plays didn't work. They try to find out why certain maneuvers succeeded and why other schemes failed. They try to find out how to correct the flaws in unsuccessful strategies, and even how to improve on successful ones. Their coaches can use these game films to illustrate any lessons they might have for their players. It's all there in living slow-motion.

As a stand-up comedian, you have access to "game

films." You should learn something each time you step onstage. Each performance can tell you what you must improve and how to improve it.

I know some performers who tape each of their performances and then carefully review them joke by joke, noting their delivery and the audience response. Some even make videotapes of their appearances and analyze these. This is fine if you have the wherewithal to make audio or video tapes of each performance and if you have the time and patience to review each and every minute of your shows.

If you can't, you might have an associate with a script outline make notes from the audience or backstage. Then you and that person can review your performance from those notes.

Even less complicated, you can review each of your performances in your own head. You can try to recall high points of your act and the slow periods. You can try to remember where the jokes played like gangbusters and where the pace slowed.

Television shows are constantly reviewing "game films" of the script. It begins with the first table-reading. The performers sit down and read the script through from cover to cover. The producers and writers are present, making notes.

Immediately after that first reading, the performers, producers, and writers review the performance. The cast indicates lines that felt unnatural to them or lines that they think can be improved. Everyone notes areas that seemed weak. Complaints and suggestions are tossed out freely, noted, and the writing staff works to repair the script.

Next, after a few days of rehearsal with the new script pages, the cast performs a run-through. That's a rehearsal in which the actors do the role on their feet with minimum props and stage dressing. Again, everyone involved reviews the performance. What needs strengthening? Which lines should be funnier? Which dialogue feels out of place? Where is the performance slowing down? The problem areas are discussed, noted, and again the writing staff makes fixes.

The process continues even on the taping day. Most shows will tape both their dress rehearsal in the afternoon and their final air performance in the evening. The "dress" and "air" shows should be identical because in post-production editing, parts of both performances will be cut together for the final tape to be broadcast.

Nevertheless, in the hour or so between the tapings, the cast and creative staff hold another meeting to discuss weaknesses and strengths in the script. The writing staff makes quick cuts, trims, and fixes and distributes the changes to the performers so they can be aware of them and quickly rehearse for the final performance.

The purpose of all these meetings, discussions, and script changes is to make the show better. The creative people know that they can learn from each show. Each time they get feedback of any kind, it can help the finished product. All of them are constantly reviewing what they just did so that they can strengthen its effectiveness the next time they do it.

Now some of you may have noted an apparent discrepancy here. If we tape both shows completely and then intercut between them, why should we worry about cuts and trims when we could just as easily do that in the editing room?

Again, we want to make the show more entertaining. We want to get good studio-audience response. That not only sounds better on the finished tape, but it lifts the actors' spirits, gives a boost to their performances.

Often the weaker parts of the show, the slower parts, are hurting the portions of the script that are working. Because of some of these weak or slow portions, we could be losing the audience. By being there, they might minimize the effectiveness of the stronger parts of the show.

Sure, we could cut those out in editing, but we'd still be left with a presentation that is affected by them. By cutting them out in the live show, we get a broadcast tape that is more vibrant, more alive.

Basically, that's the reason for all these meetings, for reviewing the "game films" so often. It makes the overall production better. That's why it's beneficial for you to do the same thing—review your presentation as often as possible. Review it on tape, with notes of a friend, or simply through recall.

Not all of this analytical study is to find faults in your act. It can also indicate strengths that you should maximize.

In working on the Bob Hope shows, I noticed that we always got big laughs when one of the guest stars would innocently put Bob Hope down. It was a sure-fire device. So any time we needed to give a guest a punch line, we'd use that gimmick.

For example, Lana Turner once visited the Bob Hope Show. She said, "Bob, I've been hearing a lot about your love scenes."

Hope feigned modesty, turned to the audience, and said, "Oh, it's nothing."

Lana said, "That's what I heard."

Knowing that this formula worked enabled us to use it more and give our guest stars a few big laughs. Studying which joke forms work best for you can help improve your act, too.

What sort of elements are you looking for as you review each performance?

Gauge the Overall Effectiveness of Your Act.

Did the audience respond enthusiastically at the end or was it just polite applause? Did they not respond at all? Keep in mind that you can learn as much from a bad performance as from a good one. You can learn something about yourself, your delivery, and your material each time you face an audience.

Once you judge the response, you want to find out why you got the reaction you did. Was it your fault? The audience's fault? The material's fault? And be honest. The purpose of this exercise is not to explain away any poor performances or to take a few more bows for the good ones; it's to improve the next one. The purpose is to learn more about what you're doing and how you're doing it.

When I worked in industry, I used to get annoyed at emergency meetings we would have to solve a customer's problem. Each department representative would come to the meeting with documents prepared to show that this problem wasn't their fault. We'd argue back and forth over who was to blame. None of this got to the heart of the problem; none of it solved the customer's complaint. We should have uncovered the problem and solved it for the customer and then, if necessary, decided which department was at fault.

Isolate Slow Portions of Your Performance.

Find out where they are and why they're slow. Once you have that information, you can create ways to revitalize them.

I once did a few shows in which I kidded some of the people I worked with. One gentleman who was prominent in the routines used to drink a touch too much at company parties. When he did, he always took his glasses off and put them in his pocket. I did a joke about him: I said, "I was talking to Charley's wife before the show and I said, 'After twenty-five years of marriage, you must know that Charley's had a little too much to drink anytime he comes home without his glasses on.' And she said, 'What glasses?'"

It was a nice joke and usually got a big laugh from

the audience. However, it took a long time to explain that Charley drank a little too much at the parties and that when he did, he took his glasses off and put them away and that he was married to his wife for twenty-five years. It was slow.

After analyzing it, it became apparent that I had to do something to enliven that buildup. So I wrote some jokes about Charley's drinking and glasses and marriage. These weren't the blockbuster jokes, but they speeded up that portion of the show that needed it, so they helped the overall effectiveness of the routine.

Of course, this doesn't mean that every slow portion of your routine is bad. Sometimes, those are there for effect, they strengthen the punch line. Jack Benny often worked slow and then delivered a solid laugh that justified the wait. No, you're looking for parts of your act that are slow and diminish the overall power of your performance. Those you want to help.

Search Out Jokes That Aren't Working.

Nothing slows an act down more than punch lines that fail. Some punch lines are sure-fire; they work every night with every audience. Some are question marks. They work gloriously on occasion and fail miserably every so often. Those you might want to keep in—help them if you can— but keep them in because when they pay off, they're worth it. Others, though, just fail. They can be great jokes, but they fail to get a response.

Most comics have gags like that. I've had some lines that I thought were hilarious and clever and innovative and a few other adjectives that I can't think of immediately. The comic who delivered them felt the same. No audience ever agreed with us. The joke would die at each performance. I'd plead with the comedian to try it again, give it another shot. He'd say, "I've given it every chance. It just doesn't work." So we'd lose it.

The joke may be perfectly constructed and, in your opinion, gloriously funny. If it doesn't work, though, it doesn't work. It has to go.

You must look at your gags with an unbiased eye. You must be cold-bloodedly realistic.

Be on the Lookout for Any Surprises.

Are there any places where the audience reaction changes abruptly? Can you discover why it does?

Once, I did a piece of material for a nightclub comedian that was a take-off on the Kennedy family. This was back when John Kennedy was just elected President, and it told of the Kennedy Dynasty as if it were the story of Cinderella. We referred to one Kennedy as the "Fairy Godfather." Without our realizing it, the audience considered this a homosexual reference and they didn't care for it. We eventually dropped the routine.

On the other hand, you might find that some devices work much better than you'd ever expect them to work. One time, I did a piece of material that struck one lady in the audience very funny. She cackled . . . loudly. Throughout the routine, I'd say to her, "You know what I'm talking about, lady." She laughed louder and the audience laughed along with her.

I stayed around for the dance that was held after the show, and throughout the evening I heard this catchphrase being used—"You know what I'm talking about, lady."

This was an isolated incident, or was it? I decided to try it again. The next time I did the routine, I picked on a guy in the audience who was laughing loudly. I asked his name, and throughout my routine I'd say, "You know what I'm talking about, Harry." It worked.

I made it a part of the routine.

You may be able to find pieces of material and shtick that can help your routine if you keep your eyes open, experiment, and review the "game films."

Find and Eliminate Offensive Material.

By this, I don't necessarily mean blue material. That may fit into this category, but it's not the only material that can be offensive. It can be almost anything.

I watched one comic perform quite well. He was scoring with good material, then suddenly the audience deserted him. He did clever routines about his childhood, his school chums, dating, and so on. They were funny and bright. Then he began talking about his divorce and his ex-wife. His routine became bitter because he was more interested in getting revenge than entertaining his audience. It made the audience feel uneasy, like visiting at a household that's in the midst of a family argument. It hurt his performance.

Now this is not to say that any material about divorce is verboten. But what it does say is that in this particular comic's case, the way he handled the situation and the material, it turned the audience against him. It hurt his act.

If he could have reviewed that and seen it, he would have changed his attitude or his material.

Look for Places to Make Cuts.

Probably one of the most effective ways to make a routine more powerful is to cut it. Eliminate the parts that keep it from being strong and funny. Cut, trim, slash, and then keep adding newer material, and you'll build a strong act eventually.

19
WORK, WORK, WORK

Professional jugglers seem to be much more courageous lately. I've seen them juggle bowling balls, razor-sharp machete knives, even operating chainsaws. And they make it look so easy, so effortless. However, they don't make it look effortless enough for me to run out to the garage and start up the chainsaw, plug in the hedge clippers, and sharpen the scythe and try to juggle them.

Even the most naive of us realizes that it takes hours of work to learn to juggle that proficiently and safely.

Probably anyone with reasonable coordination, with some effort and practice, could learn to juggle. I'm not sure of that, but I can say with certainty that no one can keep five, six, or seven balls, or knives, or chainsaws in the air the very first time. Some work, some practice is an absolute necessity.

Comedy, when it's done well, looks effortless, too. It looks easy, so people assume they can just step onstage and be hilarious with no preparation, no experience, no practice, no rehearsal. It can't be done.

Someone once said of the guitar that it was an easy instrument to play, but a difficult instrument to play well. That's because practically anyone can pick up a guitar, learn a few basic chords, and strum along to hundreds of songs. To master the guitar, though, takes study and practice. It takes devotion and dedication. In short, it takes work.

Anyone can step onstage during an open mike night and act crazy enough to get a few laughs from the audience. But to master the intricacies of comedy and to become a polished performer takes study and practice. It takes devotion and dedication. In short, it takes work.

There is work involved at all levels of comedy. It takes study and analyzation to discover who is doing what in the field. It takes research to know what the audiences are responding to. It takes considerable effort to assemble, polish, and perfect your material. Then, it takes rehearsal time to perfect your delivery. It requires effort to hone your act and your delivery.

It takes all of this work to make your comedy appear spontaneous and effortless.

This work is not just a sham to convince yourself that you're doing all that you can to succeed in comedy. It has honest-to-goodness practical benefits.

It Makes You as Good as You Can Be.

Remember way back in Chapter 1 that I offered you a magic bullet that would guarantee success? That magic bullet was to be good. That was it. Be good and you'll be successful—in comedy and, in fact, in any other profession you try. Be good.

The only way to get to be good is to work at your craft. Spend time in study and practice. Work to eliminate your weak points and improve even your strong points. It's work that makes you better and better and eventually so good that you can't be ignored. You'll be noticed, rewarded, and that equals success.

It Gives You an Edge on Your Competition.

There's a television commercial airing now that features

Jim Courier, the outstanding young tennis professional. The commercial shows Courier out hitting balls early in the morning, then jogging several miles. It shows him working with weights to develop strength, and then out hitting more tennis balls. We see him doing stretching exercises and tossing the medicine ball back and forth with a partner. Then he asks himself, "Are the other tennis players working this hard? Geez, I hope not."

Tennis is fiercely competitive and it rewards the winner. Those who finish first in the tournaments get the bulk of the money, they become millionaires both through prize money and lucrative endorsements. The also-rans get what's left over.

Comedy, too, is fiercely competitive. It rewards the winners and doles out just enough to the also-rans. How do you guarantee that you'll be among the winners? The same way Jim Courier demonstrates in that video advertisement. You work harder than the rest of the field. You work feverishly and get so much better than the rest that you leave them in the pack as you become a standout.

It Builds Confidence.

When you get in your car in the morning, you don't fret. You just slam the door, hook up your seatbelt, turn on the ignition, pull into traffic, and go on your merry way. You're getting into a vehicle that weighs thousands of pounds and will travel at speeds of maybe sixty miles an hour or more. You'll be weaving in and out of other cars going that fast or faster, passing within a few feet of speeding vehicles going in the opposite direction, and you do it all calmly.

Why? Because you know what you're doing behind the wheel of a car. You've done it hundreds of times before, and you're confident that you can handle any situation that might arise. You're a good driver and you know it.

I'm always amazed at how cool basketball players are

when they have to sink critical free throws at the end of a game. They step up to the foul line with the opposing fans shouting and waving pennants to distract them, and they calmly make the shots. I'm awed at how well figure skaters, under pressure, can execute the spins and jumps. I'm intrigued at how routinely policemen react to potentially dangerous situations.

All of these people are confident because they've practiced these things many times. They've trained for them. The work they've done has convinced them that they will perform just as well as they can regardless of the pressure.

In Chapter 2 we talked about the confidence that a performer needs. You owe it to yourself, your act, and your audience to be so well prepared when you step to the microphone that you can be as cool as the basketball player, the figure skater, or the cop on patrol.

When you've worked hard, prepared yourself, and rehearsed, you'll know that you are going to be as good as you can possibly be. You can entertain an audience as calmly as you get in your car and drive to the theatre.

It Can Inspire You to Go Further.

Hard work produces results. Results produce enthusiasm. Enthusiasm produces even more hard work and more and better results.

When I was in high school, a friend of mine played pretty good banjo. At our school picnics and cookouts, he could listen to any song and play along with it. I thought he was a fabulous musician. One day he offered to teach me to play the banjo.

I declined. I didn't want to make a fool of myself. I told him, "I can't read music and I don't know anything about music." He insisted that I learn just three chords. He patiently showed me how to finger them on the fingerboard and he insisted that I practice them.

I did, but reluctantly. It was difficult. My fingers didn't

want to bend that way, and even when I got them where they were supposed to go, the music I made sounded dead. Besides, I thought, this isn't music; this is only three chords.

Eventually though, under his prodding, I got pretty good at strumming those three chords. At the next school picnic, he and I played the banjo together. He would shout out the chord as we played, and I'd quickly switch my fingering. I could play along with him to hundreds of tunes.

It was actually fun and I discovered that after a while, I didn't need my mentor to shout out which chords I should play. I began to be able to hear the chord changes in the music.

Here's the interesting phenomenon, though. I now wanted my teacher to show me how to play more difficult chords and how to play more complicated pieces of music.

When I worked hard enough to master these three basic chords, I wanted to learn more. I wanted to work even harder to become a better and better banjo player. Working at your craft will do the same for you. You'll discover that with some effort, you can do things you doubted you could ever do. That will inspire you to try even more.

You'll surprise yourself at just how much you can learn and how much talent you do have.

It Impresses Other People.

Years ago, I wrote a magazine article about the business of comedy writing. After it appeared, many people wrote and asked for my help in getting into television writing. I wrote to them with a list of things that I wanted them to do. One wrote back to me and said, "I did all of that, what do I do next?" I had no idea. No one had ever gotten that far before.

I worked with this gentleman, coaching him and giving him additional assignments. He did every one of them and completed them all on time. Soon he was writing professionally; shortly after that he got into television writing, and has enjoyed a long and profitable career in comedy.

Was he the most talented of the people who wrote and asked for my advice? I don't know. Was he the most successful? Yes. Why? Because he did the work, and that impressed me enough to not only help him, but also recommend him to some producers who were looking for writers.

I met another aspiring writer who asked for help in her young career. I asked what she had written. She rattled off several nightclub clients, a weekly newspaper column, a few sitcom scripts she had written on spec, and a few other pieces of comedy writing she had completed. I said, "You don't need me. Just keep doing what you're doing and you'll make it." And she did—very soon after that.

I had not seen any of her writing, but she worked so hard at her craft that I "knew" she wouldn't be denied. She wasn't. Her hard work impressed several comedians, producers, and even book publishers.

Another young writer I knew had submitted some hour-long scripts to an agent. The agent thought the writing had potential, but wanted to see some half-hour sitcom scripts, too. He asked the writer to create spec scripts for two popular sitcoms that were currently on TV.

Within a few weeks, the writer called back and said, "I have the two scripts completed. Would you like to read them." The agent said, "I don't really have to see them. I'm just impressed that you finished them."

Most of the people who are in the comedy industry worked hard to get there. They appreciate the value of effort. They recognize the benefit of hard work. When you exhibit that sort of productivity, it will pay dividends with the people who count.

My former writing partner believed (and he eventually convinced me) that if anyone wanted to write television comedy, all he or she had to do was write, write, and keep writing and that person would soon become a television writer.

Your hard work will not only make you better and better at the craft of comedy, but it will eventually impress someone who counts.

It's Good Training.

The original *Rocky* movie dramatizes the benefits of hard work. Rocky Balboa was a club fighter, an amateur. Nevertheless, the World Champion wanted to give him a shot at the title and promote it heavily. Rocky at first resisted. He knew he wasn't good enough to fight the top heavyweight in the world, but then he changed his mind. He was going to take this one shot at success even though it was a long shot, but he was going to work hard and prepare.

He jogged all over the streets of Philadelphia with inspiring music being played under his efforts. He whipped himself into great shape, and the climax was when he jogged up the steps of the Philadelphia Art Museum with the music playing loudly and he danced around up there with his arms raised in jubilation.

But wait a minute. What does jogging have to do with boxing? Boxing requires timing, finesse, strategy, strength. Jogging is just running.

Yet all boxers do roadwork. They work out in the ring, they jump rope, and they run for miles. Why? They do it because it builds stamina. It gives them staying power.

Throwing punches at an opponent who is hitting back is exhausting work. To do it for ten or twelve rounds is incredibly fatiguing. That's when the effort of the roadwork pays off. It's good training for staying in the ring and fighting until the final bell.

Success can be exhausting, too. In fact, the more success you achieve, the harder you'll have to work. Not only is more expected of you when you gain some fame, but also more people will be rooting for your collapse.

Sometimes staying on top is harder than getting there, but we'll talk more about that in the following chapter.

Working hard on your career now not only helps you get where you're going, but it's excellent training for the stamina you'll need once you get there. All of your effort will pay dividends down the line.

20
WHY DON'T YOU STAY AWHILE?

When I was a kid, the local authorities decided to renovate a park in our neighborhood. We youngsters discovered a pile of fresh gravel that stood about fifteen feet high. It was more inviting and challenging than the rusting swings and rotting benches that were there before. Someone shouted "King of the Hill" and my pals all began scrambling to the top of the gritty mountain.

I had never heard of this game, but the rules became readily apparent—one kid would get to the summit and everyone else would try to topple him from it.

I learned that getting to the top was relatively easy. Hardly anyone bothered you en route. They all ignored you in their scramble to the top. However, once you got there, everyone was your enemy. All of your buddies now tried to toss you off the peak.

It's similar in the stand-up comedy field. Achieving success is easier than maintaining it. Show-business wisdom warns, "You're only as good as your last show."

All of us can think of people who blazed onto the comedy scene, glowed brightly for a while, and then disappeared. Someone once said: "It's better to be a 'has-been' than a 'never-was.'" That may be true, but the best option is to be a "still-am."

The struggle to achieve success in stand-up comedy takes time and effort. It takes work, study, diligence, perseverance. Once you achieve it, you'll want to enjoy it for some time—like forever.

Following are a few tips to help you remain "King of the Hill."

Be Good.

In Chapter 1 I offered this advice as the "magic bullet" that would insure success. Now I offer it as the primary formula that will maintain your success. Quality is one success gimmick that will stand up to any litmus test. If you lie, cheat, steal, smooth talk, or bamboozle your way to achievement, you can be discovered, exposed. Excellence, though, will stand on its own merit.

A friend of mine puts it in a down-home way: "Dance with who brung you to the party." You reached the top of your profession because you were good. Stay good and you'll stay on top.

Success brings many perks—you make money, you enjoy fame, you ride in limos, you meet stars—but none of these allow you the luxury of relaxing your standards. You must be good.

Actually, you should get better. When you acquire some fame, more is expected of you and more people are out to topple you. When I worked in industry, a co-worker was promoted to manager. The announcement was made first to those of us who worked in his department. He was a friend and a co-worker; now he'd be our boss. People filed by to congratulate him. I shook his hand and said, "Congratulations. I never liked you anyway."

It was a friendly joke, but with a bit of universal truth within. People can be resentful, jealous, envious of your success. And even those who aren't can still be fiercely competitive. In Western movies, everyone wants to shoot it out with the fastest draw. In sports, the underdogs play harder against the perennial champions. And they can play with reckless abandon. They have less at stake.

Being successful carries an obligation to continue to work hard to be successful. There are very few plateaus where you can stop and rest because those who don't stop will go right past you.

Update Your Act.

Someone once wise-cracked that being a comic is like being a hooker. You get paid for something, and even after you give it away, you've still got it. There's some truth to that. You do earn money for the same act night after night. Sooner or later, though, the comic is going to have to change the act.

Comedy must keep changing or it stagnates. There is nothing duller than an old joke. There is nothing less amusing than tired, old comedy material. To have zest, comedy must be fresh, inventive, original.

You'll gain recognition as a stand-up comedian because your material is new and innovative. People like it and want to listen to it. After they've heard it, though, and enjoyed it, they'll ask, "What else have you got?" That's when you'll have to ask yourself, "What else have I got?"

As I work on this book, I'm also writing a television show that will pay tribute to Bob Hope on his ninetieth birthday. Hope has enjoyed a show-business career that spans eight decades. He began in vaudeville, then adapted for Broadway, films, radio, television, nightclubs, and concerts. Even in his nineties, Bob Hope is constantly seeking creative ideas and different material.

When Gallagher celebrates his ninetieth birthday, he won't be doing his "sledge-o-matic" routine. It's a funny bit and one that audiences love. It's the gimmick that got Gallagher noticed and it has served him well, but it won't and shouldn't last forever.

Comics change. They have to. Bill Cosby began by talking about his childhood experiences. He does other routines now. Jack Benny was known in his vaudeville days as a "rapid-fire comedian." Certainly, when he matured into the legendary radio and television comedian, he worked slowly and deliberately. Whoopi Goldberg, Billy Crystal, and Robin Williams in their relatively short comedy careers have changed their style and their material noticeably.

George Burns and Gracie Allen were hits on radio from the day they started. Their broadcasts were always high in the ratings. Then they suddenly began to slip. George Burns spoke to the writers and said, "We've got to change. We're not young kids anymore." They were still doing jokes about George Burns trying to impress a young and naive Gracie. In fact, they were married and had youngsters of their own. Burns suggested that the stories and the jokes reflect those changes. When they did, the ratings zoomed upward again and they remained a top-rated show until Gracie retired.

One gimmick can help you attain success, but constant updating and revitalization will keep you on top.

Be Willing and Ready to Accept Change.

If there is one constant in our world, it is change. Times change, attitudes change, audiences change, the business changes, and you change.

In the previous section, we discussed how you must change your material and delivery, update it. However, you should also be ready to accept any change that might come your way.

Stars like Roseanne Arnold, Tim Allen, Jerry Seinfeld, and others were stand-up comics. They worked nightclubs. Then the fates offered them a situation-comedy format. They earned a lot of money and fame by being ready to accept that change.

Bob Newhart has had a long, successful career as a television actor. He's headlined two very successful situation comedies and is working on his third one this sea-son. Would his career as a nightclub comic have survived this long and this successfully?

Richard Belzer was a stand-up comic who gained some notoriety in the comedy clubs and on television. Now he's starring in a dramatic role on "Homicide."

Will Rogers did rope tricks before converting to one-line comedy. Bob Hope began as a song-and-dance man in vaudeville and on Broadway. The stand-up comedy came later. W.C. Fields began as a juggler. Johnny Carson started out as a magician.

The fates are unpredictable and may offer opportunities where we would never think to look for them. Being open to these opportunities can extend and sometimes further your career. Some experiments work out; some don't.

Time always marches on. If you insist on standing still, on doing today exactly what you did yesterday, many opportunities may be passing you by.

Don't Take Yourself Too Seriously.

You're only a comedian. You may be a rich and famous performer, but you're still only a comedian. You tell jokes and people laugh—that's about it.

Of course, you're also a person with friends, family, and interests. You may care deeply about certain things—political and social issues. That's good. The more you care about others, the more incisive your comedy can be.

However, you must be careful to keep your personal philosophies in balance and perspective. You're hired to tell jokes and not to preach. Regardless of your private convictions, as a comedian, your primary purpose is to make people laugh.

Toward the end of the eleven-year run of "The Carol Burnett Show," Carol used to reject well-written sketches because they weren't meaningful enough. "It's only a funny sketch," Carol would say. She wanted a message embedded in each one.

Funny sketches made Carol famous and rich. Promoting causes didn't. If an occasional sketch could also make a statement, fine. However, not every sketch could or should.

Some of you may be rebelling now. You may say, "Wait a minute. If I have something important to say, why shouldn't I say it? Being a comedian shouldn't rule that out." Let me explain the danger.

You can easily progress from "funny" to "funny with a message" to "message only." You cease being a comedian and become a preacher. It kills the comedy.

Lenny Bruce was a magnificently funny man. Many of today's comics feel that he not only inspired them, but also opened many doors for them. However, because he was so radically different and outspoken, he got in trouble with the authorities. His act was shut down several times, and he was arrested for indecent performances. He fought the persecution and is considered a pioneer, even a martyr, by today's comedians. However, he'd sometimes get so caught up in his legal battles that he'd go onstage and talk about only those—no comedy, no jokes, no humorous insight. He wasn't performing comedy behind the mike. He became a crusader rather than an entertainer.

This doesn't mean that you should ignore your beliefs totally. If you can take your causes and work them into entertaining, funny routines, do it. But remember that you're a comic. Your primary job is to be funny.

Sometimes, too, you can get your message across by example as opposed to sermonizing. My partner and I discovered that almost every sketch we wrote for "The Carol Burnett Show" ended with violence. We'd push Tim Conway out a window, shoot Harvey Korman, or blow up the entire cast and set. We were showing more mayhem on our comedy show than some detective shows. Eventually, we made a pact with ourselves that we would find more creative, humane ways to end our sketches.

We wrote sketches without violence. We didn't write sketches that preached anti-violence.

Success, too, affords one many perks. People begin to idolize you, pamper you. However, you're still just you—richer, more famous, more coddled—but still just plain, old, simple you.

Being able to keep that straight in your head can benefit your show-business longevity.

Don't Do Anything Dumb.

Nobility has its obligations. Show-business nobility, too, has responsibilities. As you gain notoriety, you have obligations to yourself, your craft, your audience, and your profession.

Careers can be destroyed by dumb actions or statements. Be wary. The more you are in the public eye, the easier it is for a slip of the tongue or an unthinking action to have serious repercussions.

Al Campanis was fired by the Los Angeles Dodgers because he said something unwise on "Nightline." Marge Schott was suspended from baseball for inconsiderate remarks.

I knew of one writer who showed up for a meeting intoxicated. Several times when his name was mentioned for a staff writing job on other shows, the response was, "No. He's a drunk."

There's a constant danger of living in the fishbowl of celebrity. Your statements and actions are not only noticed by everyone, but magnified to unreal proportions. Be aware of that. It will help you last longer in the business.

Work for Today and for Tomorrow.

Your yesterdays got you where you are now. Today you're enjoying it. Your tomorrows are still unknown.

Today, though, is tomorrow's yesterday. That means

you must work now to secure your future success. It's wise, regardless of what level you've attained, to devote part of your present efforts to present requirements, and part to the future.

If you write a great routine for your act today, it will be outdated someday. Almost as soon as you create it, you'll have to think about replacing it. Everything you're doing today will probably be done differently in the future.

If you can maintain the quality of your present work and also prepare for the future, you'll always be ready. You'll guarantee yourself a long career.

THE LAST WORD

Comedy is a blessed profession. You're an ordinary person. You lead a commonplace life in which everyday events occur. The same is true of your listeners. Yet you can transform these events into fascinating, interesting, entertaining moments.

That's your unique skill. You have the talent to bring laughter into the ordinary. You can invent happiness.

Nothing in this book is meant to tamper with that gift. These are suggestions that might help you enhance your skills, perhaps understand them better, or to use them more effectively for greater or quicker success.

Read this book's recommendations, consider them, try them, if you like. Adopt some; adapt others; discard those that don't blend with your singular abilities.

You're the one at the microphone. You're the one with the ambition, the drive, and the talent. You're the one who has been anointed by the gods of comedy.

You have the last word.